Alternative Therapies

GEDDES&
GROSSET

This edition published 1999 by Geddes & Grosset,
an imprint of Children's Leisure Products Limited

©1997 Children's Leisure Products Limited,
David Dale House, New Lanark ML11 9DJ, Scotland

Cover photograph by J. P. Nacivet, courtesy of Telegraph Colour
Library

ISBN 1 85534 694 X

Printed and bound in the UK

Contents

Acupuncture

Origins

Acupuncture is an ancient Chinese therapy that involves inserting needles into the skin at specific points of the body. The word 'acupuncture' originated from a Dutch physician, William Ten Rhyne, who had been living in Japan during the latter part of the 17th century and it was he who introduced it to Europe. The term means literally 'prick with a needle'. The earliest textbook on acupuncture, dating from approximately 400 BC, was called *Nei Ching Su Wen*, which means 'Yellow Emperor's Classic of Internal Medicine'. Also recorded at about the same time was the successful saving of a patient's life by acupuncture, the person having been expected to die whilst in a coma. Legend has it that acupuncture was developed when it was realized that soldiers who recovered from arrow wounds were sometimes also healed of other diseases from which they were suffering. Acupuncture was very popular with British doctors in the early 1800s for pain relief and to treat fever. There was also a specific article on the successful treatment of rheumatism that appeared in *The Lancet*. Until the end of the Ching dynasty in China in 1911, acupuncture was slowly developed and improved, but then medicine from the West increased in popularity. However, more recently there has been a revival of interest and it is again widely practised throughout China. Also, nowadays the use of laser beams and electrical currents are found to give an increased stimulative effect when using acupuncture needles.

Yin and yang

The specific points of the body into which acupuncture needles are inserted are located along 'meridians'. These are the pathways or energy channels and are believed to be related to the internal organs of the body. This energy is known as *chi* (also known as *ki* or *qi*), and the needles are used to decrease or increase the flow of energy, or to unblock it if it is impeded. Traditional Chinese medicine sees the body as being comprised of two natural forces known as the *yin* and *yang*. These two forces are complementary to each other but also opposing, the yin being the female force and calm and passive and also representing the dark, cold, swelling and moisture. The yang force is the male and is stimulating and aggressive, representing the heat and light, contraction and dryness. It is believed that the cause of ailments and diseases is due to an imbalance of these forces in the body, e.g. if a person is suffering from a headache or hypertension then this is because of an excess of yang. If, however, there is an excess of yin, this might result in tiredness, feeling cold and fluid retention.

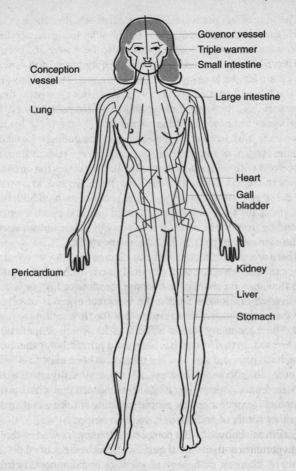

The meridians

Govenor vessel
Triple warmer
Small intestine

Conception vessel

Lung

Large intestine

Heart

Gall bladder

Pericardium

Kidney

Liver

Stomach

The aim of acupuncture is to establish whether there is an imbalance of yin and yang and to rectify it by using the needles at certain points on the body. Traditionally there were 365 points but more have been found in the intervening period and nowadays there can be as many as 2,000. There are 14 meridians (12 of which are illustrated on page 9), called after the organs they represent, e.g. the lung, kidney, heart and stomach as well as two organs unknown in orthodox medicine—the triple heater or warmer, which relates to the activity of the endocrine glands and the control of temperature. In addition, the pericardium is concerned with seasonal activity and also regulates the circulation of the blood. Of the 14 meridians, there are two, known as the *du,* or governor, and the *ren*, or conception, which both run straight up the body's midline, although the du is much shorter, extending from the head down to the mouth, while the ren starts at the chin and extends to the base of the trunk.

There are several factors that can change the flow of chi and they can be of an emotional, physical or environmental nature. The flow may be changed to become too slow or fast, or it can be diverted or blocked so that the incorrect organ is involved and the acupuncturist has to ensure that the flow returns to normal. There are many painful afflictions for which acupuncture can be used. In the West, it has been used primarily for rheumatism, back pain and arthritis, but it has also been used to alleviate other disorders such as stress, allergy, colitis, digestive troubles, insomnia, asthma, etc. It has been claimed that withdrawal symptoms (experienced by people stopping smoking and ceasing other forms of addiction) have been helped as well.

Qualified acupuncturists complete a training course of three years duration and also need qualifications in the related disciplines of anatomy, pathology, physiology and diagnosis before they can belong to a professional association. It is very important that a fully qualified acupuncturist, who is a member of the relevant professional body, is consulted because at the present time any unqualified person can use the title 'acupuncturist'.

The treatment

At a consultation, the traditional acupuncturist uses a set method of ancient rules to determine the acupuncture points. The texture and colouring of the skin, type of skin, posture and movement and the tongue will all be examined and noted, as will the patient's voice. These different factors are all needed for the Chinese diagnosis. A number of questions will be asked concerning the diet, amount of exercise taken, lifestyle, fears and phobias, sleeping patterns and reactions to stress. Each wrist has six pulses, and each of these stands for a main organ and its function. The pulses are felt (known as palpating), and by this means acupuncturists are able to diagnose any problems relating to the flow of chi and if there is any disease present in the internal organs. The first consultation may last an hour, especially if detailed questioning is necessary along with the palpation.

The needles used in acupuncture are disposable and made of a fine stainless steel and come already sealed in a sterile pack. They can be sterilized by the acupuncturist in a machine known as an autoclave but using boiling water is not adequate for this purpose. (Diseases such as HIV and hepatitis can be passed on by using unsterilized needles.) Once the needle is inserted into the skin it is twisted between the acupuncturist's thumb and forefinger to spread or draw the energy from a point. The depth to which the needle is inserted can vary from just below the skin to up to 12mm (half an inch) and different sensations may be felt, such as a tingling around the area of insertion or a loss of sensation at that point. Up to 15 needles can be used but

11

around five are generally sufficient. The length of time that they are left in varies from a few minutes to half an hour, and this is dependent on a number of factors, such as how the patient has reacted to previous treatment and the ailment from which he or she is suffering.

Patients can generally expect to feel an improvement after four to six sessions of therapy, the beneficial effects occurring gradually, particularly if the ailment has obvious and long-standing symptoms. Other diseases such as asthma will probably take longer before any definite improvement is felt. It is possible that some patients may not feel any improvement at all, or even feel worse after the first session, and this is probably because of the energies in the body being over-stimulated. To correct this, the acupuncturist will gradually use fewer needles and for a shorter period of time. If no improvement is felt after about six to eight treatments, then it is doubtful whether acupuncture will be of any help. For general body maintenance and health, most traditional acupuncturists suggest that sessions be arranged at the time of seasonal changes.

How does it work?

There has been a great deal of research, particularly by the Chinese who have produced many books detailing a high success rate for acupuncture in treating a variety of disorders. These results are, however, viewed cautiously in the West as methods of conducting clinical trials vary from East to West. Nevertheless, trials have been carried out in the West, and it has been discovered that a pain message can be stopped from reaching the brain by using acupuncture. The signal would normally travel along a nerve but it is possible to 'close a gate' on the nerve, thereby preventing the message from reaching the brain, hence preventing the perception of pain. Acupuncture is believed to work by blocking the pain signal. However, doctors stress that pain can be a warning that something is wrong or of the occurrence of a particular disease, such as cancer, that requires an orthodox remedy or method of treatment.

It has also been discovered that there are substances produced by the body that are connected with pain relief. These substances are called endorphins and encephalins, and they are natural opiates. Studies from all over the world show that acupuncture stimulates the release of these opiates into the central nervous system, thereby giving pain relief. The amount of opiates released has a direct bearing on the degree of pain relief. Acupuncture is a widely used form of anaesthesia in China where, for suitable patients, it is said to be extremely effective (90 per cent). It is used successfully during childbirth, dentistry and for operations. Orthodox doctors in the West now accept that heat treatment, massage and needles used on a sensitive part of the skin afford relief from pain caused by disease elsewhere. These areas are known as trigger points, and they are not always situated close to the organ that is affected by disease. It has been found that approximately three-quarters of these trigger points are the same as the points used in Chinese acupuncture. Recent research has also shown that it is possible to find the acupuncture points by the use of electronic instruments as these register less electrical resistance in areas of the skin. As yet, no evidence has been found to substantiate the existence of meridians.

Auricular therapy

Auricular therapy is a method of healing using stimulation of different acupuncture points on the surface of the ear. Auricular therapists claim that there are over 200 points on the ear that are connected to a particular organ, tissue or part of the body. If a disorder is present, its corresponding point on the ear may be sensitive or tender to touch and pressure, or there may even be some kind of physical sign such as a mark, spot or lump. Stimulation of the ear is carried out by means of acupuncture needles, or minute electric currents or a laser beam may be used.

It is claimed that auricular therapy is helpful in the treatment of various chronic conditions such as rheumatism and arthritis and also problems of addiction. During a first consultation, the auricular therapist obtains a detailed picture of the patient's state of health, lifestyle and family background. A physical examination of the ears is carried out and any distinguishing features are recorded. The therapist passes a probe over the surface of the ear to find any sensitive points that indicate the areas requiring treatment.

The practice of manipulating needles in the ear to cure diseases in other parts of the body is a very ancient one. It has been used for many hundreds of years in some eastern and Mediterranean countries and in China. Although the method of action is not understood, auricular therapy is becoming increasingly popular in several countries of the world including the United Kingdom.

The Alexander Technique

Breaking the habit of bad posture

The Alexander technique is a practical and simple method of learning to focus attention on movement and posture during daily activities. Frederick Mathias Alexander (1869–1955), an Australian therapist who was originally an actor, demonstrated that the difficulties many people experience in learning, in control of performance and in physical functioning are caused by unconscious habits. These habits interfere with our natural poise and our capacity to learn. When we stop interfering with the innate coordination of the body, we can take on more complex activities with greater self-confidence and presence of mind. It is about learning to bring into our conscious awareness the choices we make as we make them. Gentle hands-on and verbal instruction reveal the underlying principles of human coordination, allow the student to experience and observe his or her own habitual patterns and give the means for release and change.

Armouring

Most of us are unconsciously armouring ourselves in relation to our environment. This is hard work and often leaves us feeling anxious, alienated, depressed and unlovable. Armouring is a deeply unconscious behaviour that has probably gone on since early childhood, maybe even since infancy. Yet it is a habit we can unlearn in the present through careful self-observation. We can unlearn our use of excess tension in our thoughts, movements and relationships.

Correct posture

The Alexander technique is based on correct posture so that the body is able to function naturally and with the minimum amount of muscular effort. As an actor Alexander found that he was losing his voice when performing but that after rest his condition temporarily improved. Although he received medical help, the condition was not permanently cured, and it occurred to him that while he was acting he might be doing something that caused the problem. To see what this might be, he performed in front of a mirror and saw what happened when he was about to speak. He experienced difficulty in breathing and lowered his head, thus making himself shorter. He realized that the strain of remembering his lines and having to project his voice so that the people farthest away in the audience would be able to hear was causing him a great deal of stress and that the way he reacted was a quite natural reflex action. In fact, even thinking about having to project his voice made the symptoms recur, and from this he concluded that there must be a close connection between body and mind. He was determined to try to improve the situation and gradually, by watching and altering his stance and posture and his mental attitude to his performance on stage, matters improved. He was able to act and speak on stage and use his body in a more relaxed and natural fashion.

In 1904 Alexander travelled to London where he had decided to let others know about his method of retraining the body. He soon became very popular with other actors who appreciated the benefits of using his technique. Other public figures, such as the author Aldous Huxley, also benefited. Later he went to America, achieving considerable success and international recognition for his technique. At the age of 78 he suffered a stroke, but by using his method he managed to regain the use of all his faculties—an achievement that amazed his doctors.

The treatment

The Alexander technique is said to be completely harmless, encouraging an agreeable state between mind and body, and is also helpful for a number of disorders such as headaches and back pain. Today, Alexander training schools can be found all over the world. A simple test to determine if people can benefit is to observe their posture. People frequently do not even stand correctly, and this can encourage aches and pains if the body is unbalanced. It is incorrect to stand with round shoulders or to slouch. This often looks uncomfortable and discomfort may be felt. Sometimes people will hold themselves too erect and unbending, which again can have a bad effect. The correct posture and balance for the body needs the least muscular effort and the body will be aligned correctly. When walking one should not slouch, hold the head down or have the shoulders stooped. The head should be balanced correctly above the spine with the shoulders relaxed. It is suggested that the weight of the body should be felt being transferred from one foot to the other whilst walking.

Once a teacher has been consulted, all movements and how the body is used will be observed. Many muscles are used in everyday activities, and over the years bad habits can develop unconsciously, with stress also affecting the use of muscles. This can be demonstrated in people gripping a pen with too much force or holding the steering wheel of a car too tightly whilst driving. Muscular tension can be a serious problem affecting some people when the head, neck and back are forced out of line, which in turn leads to rounded shoulders with the

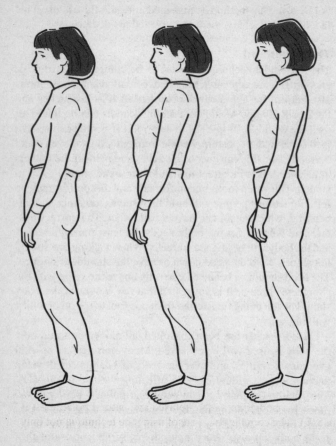

Slouching   Too unbending   Correct posture

head held forward and the back curved. If this situation is not altered and the body is not re-aligned correctly, the spine will become curved with a hump possibly developing. This leads to back pain and puts a strain on internal organs such as the chest and lungs.

An Alexander teacher guides a person, as he or she moves, to use less tension. The instructor works by monitoring the student's posture and reminding him or her to implement tiny changes in movement to eradicate the habit of excess tension. Students learn to stop bracing themselves up or to stop collapsing into themselves. As awareness grows, it becomes easier to recognize and relinquish the habit of armouring and dissolve the artificial barriers we put between ourselves and others.

An analogy of this process can be seen in the now familiar three-dimensional Magic Eye Art. With our ordinary way of looking we see only a mass of dots. When we shift to the 'Magic Eye' way of seeing, a three-dimensional object appears. Through the Alexander technique a similar type of experience is available, but the three-dimensional object we experience in this case is ourselves.

No force is used by the teacher other than some gentle manipulation to start students off correctly. Some teachers use light pushing methods on the back and hips, etc, while others might first ensure that the student is relaxed and then pull gently on the neck, which stretches the body. Any bad postures will be corrected by the teacher, and the student will be shown how best to alter this so that muscles will be used most effectively and with the least effort. Any manipulation that is used will be to ease the body into a more relaxed and natural position. It is helpful to be completely aware of using the technique not only on the body but also with the mind. With frequent use of the Alexander technique for posture and the release of tension, the muscles and the body should be used correctly with a consequent improvement in, for example, the manner of walking and sitting.

The length of time for each lesson can vary from about half an hour to three quarters of an hour and the number of lessons is usually between 10 and 30, by which time students should have gained sufficient knowledge to continue practising the technique by themselves. Once a person has learned how to improve posture, it will be found that he or she is taller and carrying the body in a more upright manner. The technique has been found to be of benefit to dancers, athletes and those having to speak in public. Other disorders claimed to have been treated successfully are depressive states, headaches caused by tension, anxiety, asthma, hypertension, respiratory problems, colitis, osteoarthritis and rheumatoid arthritis, sciatica and peptic ulcer.

The Alexander technique is recommended for all ages and types of people as their overall quality of life, both mental and physical, can be improved. People can learn how to resist stress, and one eminent professor experienced a great improvement in a variety of ways: in quality of sleep, lessening of high blood pressure and improved mental awareness. He even found that his ability to play a musical instrument had improved.

The Alexander technique can be applied to two positions adopted every day, namely sitting in a chair and sitting at a desk. To be seated in the correct manner the head should be comfortably balanced, with no tension in the shoulders, a small gap between the knees (if legs are crossed the spine and pelvis become out of line or twisted) and the soles of the feet should be flat on the floor. It is incorrect to sit with the head lowered and the shoulders slumped forward because the stomach becomes restricted and breathing may also be affected. On the

Slumped posture

Comfortably balanced posture

Bad posture

Good balanced posture

other hand, it is also incorrect to hold the body in a stiff and erect position.

To sit correctly while working at a table, the body should be held upright but in a relaxed manner with any bending movement coming from the hips and with the seat flat on the chair. If writing, the pen should be held lightly, and if using a computer one should ensure that the arms are relaxed and feel comfortable. The chair should be set at a comfortable height with regard to the level of the desk. It is incorrect to lean forward over a desk, because this hampers breathing, or to hold the arms in a tense, tight manner.

There has been some scientific research carried out that concurs with the beliefs that Alexander formed, such as the relationship between mind and body (the thought of doing an action actually triggering a physical reaction or tension). Today, doctors do not have any opposition to the Alexander technique and may recommend it on occasions.

Although the Alexander technique does not treat specific symptoms, you can encourage a marked improvement in overall health, alertness and performance by consciously eliminating harmful habits that cause physical and emotional stress and by becoming more aware of how you engage in your activities.

Autogenic Training

Autogenic training is a form of therapy that seeks to teach the patient to relax, thereby relieving stress. This is achieved by the patient learning a series of six basic exercises that can be undertaken either lying flat on the back, sitting in an armchair or sitting towards the edge of a chair with the head bent forwards and the chin on the chest. The six exercises concentrate on: (1) breathing and respiration; (2) heartbeat; (3) the forehead to induce a feeling of coolness; (4) the lower abdomen and stomach to induce a feeling of warmth; (5) the arms and legs to induce a feeling of warmth; (6) the neck, shoulders, arms and legs to induce a feeling of heaviness.

It is now well established that a number of illnesses and disorders are related to, or made worse by, stress. By learning the techniques and exercises of autogenic training, the person is able to achieve a state of relaxation and tranquillity, will sleep better and generally has more energy and a greater feeling of wellbeing. Autogenic training is taught at group sessions involving a small number of people (usually about six).

Patients with a variety of disorders may benefit from autogenic training, which can also help people who feel under stress without particular physical symptoms. Illnesses that may be helped include irritable bowel syndrome, digestive disorders, muscular aches and cramps, ulcers, headaches and high blood pressure as well as anxieties, fears and phobias, insomnia and some other psychological illnesses. This form of therapy can benefit people of all age groups, although it is considered that children under the age of six may not be able to understand the training. Therapists in autogenic training usually hold medical or nursing qualifications and expect to obtain a full picture of the patient's state of health before treatment begins. Therapy is available both privately and through the National Health Service in some areas of the United Kingdom.

Ayurvedic Medicine

This is a holistic approach to health care that, alongside orthodox medicine, is a major form of therapy in India and is gain-
ing an increasing number of followers in Western countries. A
great deal of emphasis is placed on preventative measures to
maintain good health. Hence the practitioner in Ayurvedic medicine obtains a detailed picture of all aspects of the patient's life
and has frequent consultations with the person. If any aspect of
the patient's life undergoes a change the practitioner may ad-
vise some form of treatment to prevent any problems from occurring. Methods of treatment include a great variety of medicines that are derived from plant and mineral sources, meditation, yoga and other exercises, religious ceremonies, water and
steam baths, massage and specially planned diets.

In the Ayurvedic philosophy, everything in life is held to be
controlled by three forces which are called *pitta*, *vata* and *kapha*.
Pitta is said to be like the sun, a great source of energy and in
control of all metabolic processes and bodily functions. Vata
resembles the wind, which is a continual source of movement
and controls the workings of the brain and nervous system.
Kapha is like the moon and its tidal influences, and controls the
fluids of the body and the growth and regeneration of cells.
Also, in Ayurvedic medicine all disorders are grouped into four
broad categories (although a holistic approach is still maintained). These are: (1) mental, covering disorders or symptoms
with an emotional basis, especially the stronger feelings such
as jealousy, fears and phobias, hatred, rage and depression; (2)
physical, covering most illnesses and internal disorders; (3)

accidental, covering illnesses and disorders that are caused by some form of external trauma; (4) natural disorders or symptoms that are particularly associated with certain ages or stages in life.

In Ayurvedic medicine it is believed that good health results from the three forces of pitta, kapha and vata being balanced and in harmony with one another. If one force becomes relatively stronger or weaker than the others, then disorder arises, causing symptoms of illness. A person 'inherits' his or her own particular balance of forces at the moment of conception. Imbalance in any of the three forces may arise as a result of stressful life events or because of a lack of care in maintaining the balance.

There are an increasing number of practitioners of Ayurvedic medicine in Great Britain. Many believe that its greatest strength lies in its emphasis on the maintenance of good health and prevention of problems or illnesses before they arise. The fact that the physician and the patient need to have a close working relationship no doubt provides reassurance for many of the followers of Ayurvedic medicine.

Chiropractic

Origins

The word 'chiropractic' originates from two Greek words, *kheir*, which means 'hand', and *praktikos*, which means 'practical'. A school of chiropractic was established in about 1895 by a healer called Daniel Palmer (1845–1913). He was able to cure a man's deafness that had occurred when he bent down and felt a bone click. Upon examination Palmer discovered that some bones of the man's spine had become displaced. After successful manipulation the man regained his hearing. Palmer formed the opinion that if there was any displacement in the skeleton this could affect the function of nerves, either increasing or decreasing their action and thereby resulting in a malfunction, i.e. a disease.

Chiropractic is used to relieve pain by manipulation and to correct any problems that are present in joints and muscles, especially the spine. Like osteopathy, no use is made of surgery or drugs. If there are any spinal disorders they can cause widespread problems elsewhere in the body, such as the hip, leg or arm, and can also initiate lumbago, sciatica, a slipped disc or other back problems. It is even possible that spinal problems can result in seemingly unrelated problems such as catarrh, migraine, asthma, constipation, stress, etc. However, the majority of a chiropractor's patients suffer mainly from neck and back pain. People suffering from whiplash injuries sustained in car accidents commonly seek the help of a chiropractor. The whiplash effect is caused when the head is violently wrenched either forwards or backwards at the time of impact.

Another common problem that chiropractors treat is headaches, and it is often the case that tension is the underlying cause as it makes the neck muscles contract. Athletes can also obtain relief from injuries such as tennis elbow, pulled muscles, injured ligaments and sprains, etc. As well as the normal methods of manipulating joints, the chiropractor may decide it is necessary to use applications of ice or heat to relieve the injury.

Children can also benefit from treatment by a chiropractor, as there may be some slight accident that occurs in their early

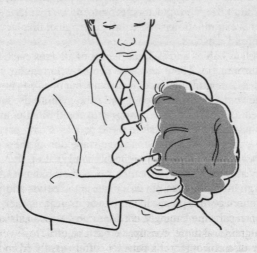

Chiropractic treatment of the neck

years that can reappear in adult life in the form of back pain. It can easily happen, for example, when a child learns to walk and bumps into furniture or when a baby falls out of a cot. This could result in some damage to the spine that will show only in adult life when a person experiences back pain. At birth, a baby's neck may be injured or the spine may be strained if the use of forceps is necessary, and this can result in headaches and neck problems as he or she grows to maturity. This early type of injury could also account for what is known as 'growing pains', when the real problem is actually damage that has been done to the bones or muscles. If a parent has any worries it is best to consult a doctor and it is possible that the child will be recommended to see a qualified chiropractor. To avoid any problems in adult life, chiropractors recommend that children have occasional examinations to detect any damage or displacement in bones and muscles.

As well as babies and children, adults of all ages can benefit from chiropractic. There are some people who regularly take painkillers for painful joints or back pain, but this does not deal with the root cause of the pain, only the symptoms that are produced. It is claimed that chiropractic could be of considerable help in giving treatment to these people. Many pregnant women experience backache at some stage during their pregnancy because of the extra weight that is placed on the spine, and they also may find it difficult keeping their balance. At the time of giving birth, changes take place in the pelvis and joints at the bottom of the spine, and this can be a cause of back pain. Lifting and carrying babies, if not done correctly, can also damage the spine and thereby make the back painful.

It is essential that any chiropractor is fully qualified and registered with the relevant professional association. At the initial visit, a patient will be asked for details of his or her case history, including the present problem, and during the examination painful and tender areas will be noted and joints will be checked to see whether they are functioning correctly or not. X-rays are frequently used by chiropractors since they can show signs of bone disease, fractures or arthritis as well as the spine's condition. After the initial visit, any treatment will normally begin as soon as the patient has been informed of the chiropractor's diagnosis. If it has been decided that chiropractic therapy will not be of any benefit, the patient will be advised accordingly.

For treatment, underwear and/or a robe will be worn and the patient will either lie, sit or stand on a specially designed couch. Chiropractors use their hands in a skilful way to effect the different manipulative techniques. If it is decided that manipulation is necessary to treat a painful lumbar joint, the patient will need to lie on his or her side. The upper and lower spine will then be rotated manually but in opposite ways. This manipulation will have the effect of partially locking the joint that is being treated and the upper leg is usually flexed to aid the procedure. The vertebra that is immediately below or above the joint will then be felt by the chiropractor, and the combination of how the patient is lying, coupled with gentle pressure applied by the chiropractor's hand, will move the joint to its farthest extent of normal movement. There will then be a very quick push applied on the vertebra, which results in its movement being extended farther than normal, ensuring that full use of the joint is regained. This is because the muscles that surround the joint are suddenly stretched, which has the effect of relaxing the muscles of the spine that work upon the joint. This alteration should cause the joint to be able to be used more naturally and should not be a painful procedure.

There can be a variety of effects felt after treatment—some

patients may feel sore or stiff or may ache for some time after the treatment while others will experience the lifting of pain at once. In some cases there may be a need for multiple treatments, perhaps four or more, before improvement is felt. On the whole, problems that have been troubling a patient for a considerable time (chronic) will need more therapy than anything that occurs quickly and is very painful (acute).

Although there is only quite a small number of chiropractors in the United Kingdom—yet this number is increasing—there is a degree of contact and liaison between them and doctors. It is generally accepted that chiropractic is an effective remedy for bone and muscular problems, and the majority of doctors would be happy to accept a chiropractor's diagnosis and treatment, although the treatment of any general diseases, such as diabetes or asthma, would not be viewed in the same manner.

Chinese Medicine

About 2500 years ago, deep in the mountains of northern China, Taoist priests practised qi gong—a meditative movement revealing and cultivating the vital life force. They believed this force, *qi* (or chi as it has become known in the West), was inseparable from life itself. They discovered that chi animated not only body and earth but was the energetic force of the entire universe. Traditional Chinese medicine is a philosophy of preserving health and is based first and foremost on an understanding of the ultimate power of chi. In contrast to much of Western medicine, traditional Chinese medicine is a preventative practice, strengthening the immune system to ward off disease.

In traditional Chinese medicine, chi is manifested both as *yin* (cold, dark and 'interior') and *yang* (warm, light and 'exterior'). In fact, chi is present in all the opposites we experience, such as night and day, hot and cold, growth and decay. And although yin and yang may be perceived as opposites, they are actually inseparable. The recognition of one is essential to the recognition of the other. The balance between them is like the motion of night and day—at the instant darkness reaches its zenith at midnight the cycle has begun to flow steadily towards dawn. At noon, the zenith of light, the day begins slowly to turn towards the darkness of night. All the internal organs of the body are subject to this nocturnal-diurnal swing of the universe.

This world view further holds that chi, manifesting as yin/yang, makes up the universe in the form of five elements: wood, fire, earth, metal and water. These five elements also represent our bodily constitution as human beings, making us one with the universe. Chi flows into our bodies, up from the earth in its yin form and down from the heavens in its yang form. The energy channels in our bodies through which it moves are called *meridians*.

These meridians do not directly correspond to any anatomical component recognized by Western medicine. The best way to understand the flow of chi through the meridians is to compare it to the flow of blood in our veins and arteries. If our blood does not reach our toes, they become dead. If our blood does not flow freely, we have high or low blood pressure. If our blood clots, we have an embolism or a stroke. Similarly, unbalanced or stagnant chi can cause many diseases and ailments. In fact, traditional Chinese medicine is based on the principle that every illness, ailment and discomfort in the body can be explained in terms of an imbalance of chi.

Each meridian is related to one of the five elements. For example, the heart meridian is related to the element fire, the kidney and bladder to water. Along the meridians are pressure points, or 'gateways', special places where chi can become blocked. With the help of a trained practitioner, its flow can be freed and balance restored.

Colour Therapy

Colour therapy uses coloured light to treat disease and disorder and to help restore good health. It is well known that human beings respond to coloured light and are affected in different ways by rays of various wavelengths. This even occurs in people who are blind, so the human body is able to respond in subtle ways to electromagnetic radiation. Colour therapists believe that each individual receives and absorbs electromagnetic radiation from the sun and emits it in a unique *aura*—a pattern of colours peculiar to that person. It is believed that the aura can be recorded on film by a photographic technique known as Kirlian photography. If disease is present, this manifests itself as a disturbance of the vibrations that form the aura, giving a distorted pattern. During a consultation, a colour therapist pays particular attention to the patient's spine as each individual vertebra is believed to reflect the condition of a particular part of the body. Hence the aura from each vertebra is believed to indicate the health of its corresponding body part. Each vertebra is believed to be related to one of the eight colours of the visible spectrum. The eight colours are repeated in their usual sequence from the top to the base of the spine.

The treatment consists of bathing the body in coloured light, with appropriate colours being decided upon by the therapist. Usually one main colour is used along with a complementary one and the light is emitted in irregular bursts. Treatment sessions last for a little less than twenty minutes and are continued for at least seven weeks. The aim is to restore the natural balance in the pattern of the aura. A therapist also advises on the use of colours in the home and of clothes and soft furnishings, etc.

In orthodox medicine it is accepted that colours exert subtle influences on people, especially affecting their state of mind and psychological wellbeing. Colour therapy may well aid healing, but there is no scientific evidence to explain the way in which this might work.

Dance and Music Therapy

Dance movement therapy

Dance movement therapy is aimed at helping people to resolve deep-seated problems by communicating with and relating to others through the medium of physical movements and dance. The ability to express deep inner feelings in 'body language' and physical movements is innate in human beings. Young children express themselves freely in this way and without inhibition, and dancing would appear to be common to all past and present races and tribes of people. However, in modern industrial societies, many people find themselves unable to communicate their problems and fears either verbally or physically and may repress them to such an extent that they become ill. Dance movement therapy aims to help people to explore, recognize and come to terms with feelings and problems that they usually repress and to communicate them to others. This therapy can help emotional, psychological and stress-related disorders, anxiety and depression, addiction, problems related to physical or sexual abuse and learning disabilities. Children who are often very responsive to this therapy may have behavioural or intellectual problems, autism or other mental and physical disabilities.

People of any age can take part in dance movement therapy as the aim is to explore gently the physical movements that are within each person's capabilities. The therapist may suggest movements but hopes to encourage patients to learn to take the initiative. Eventually some groups learn to talk over feelings and problems that have emerged through taking part and are better able to resolve them.

Dance therapy sessions are organized in some hospitals and 'drop-in' and day-care centres. This form of therapy is regarded as particularly beneficial for people who suffer from a number of disorders, particularly those with psychological and emotional problems or who are intellectually disadvantaged.

Music therapy

Making music has always been important in all cultures and societies as a means of self-expression and communication. Many people have experienced the powerful effects of music, which may stimulate feelings of excitement, tranquillity, sadness or joy. Music therapy consists of creating music, using a range of different instruments and the human voice as a means of helping people to communicate their innermost thoughts, fears and feelings.

Music therapy can help people with a variety of different disorders. It is especially valuable in helping people with intellectual impairment or learning difficulties. However, those who are physically disabled in some way may also benefit, especially people who need to improve their breathing or extend their range of movements. The sessions are conducted by a trained therapist who has a qualification in music, and the treatment may be available at some hospitals. Many therapists work in residential homes and schools, and the demand for the service greatly exceeds the number of people working in this field. The approach taken depends upon the nature of the patient's problems. If the person is a child who is intellectually impaired and who perhaps cannot talk, the therapist builds up a relationship using instruments, vocal sounds and the shared experience of music-making. With a patient who is physically disabled or who has psychological or emotional problems, a different approach with more discussion is likely to be adopted.

Since most people react in some way to music and enjoy the experience of music-making, this form of therapy is usually highly beneficial and successful. Anyone can benefit and the person need not have any previous musical ability, knowledge or experience. Music therapy is especially helpful for children with intellectual and/or physical disabilities.

Hydrotherapy

The healing quality of water

Hydrotherapy is the use of water to heal and ease a variety of ailments, and the water may be used in a number of different ways. The healing properties of water have been recognized since ancient times, notably by the Greek, Roman and Turkish civilizations but also by people in Europe and China. Most people know the benefits of a hot bath in relaxing the body, relieving muscular aches and stiffness, and helping to bring about restful sleep. Hot water or steam causes blood vessels to dilate, opens skin pores and stimulates perspiration, and relaxes limbs and muscles. A cold bath or shower acts in the opposite way and is refreshing and invigorating. The cold causes blood vessels in the skin to constrict and blood is diverted to internal tissues and organs to maintain the core temperature of the body. Applications of cold water or ice reduce swelling and bruising and cause skin pores to close.

Physiotherapy

In orthodox medicine, hydrotherapy is used as a technique of physiotherapy for people recovering from serious injuries with problems of muscle wastage. Also, it is used for people with joint problems and those with severe physical disabilities. Many hospitals also offer the choice of a water birth to expectant mothers, and this has become an increasingly popular method of childbirth. Hydrotherapy may be offered as a form of treatment for other medical conditions in *naturopathy,* using the techniques listed above. It is wise to obtain medical advice before proceeding with hydrotherapy, and this is especially important for elderly persons, children and those with serious conditions or illnesses.

Treatment techniques in hydrotherapy

Hot baths

Hot baths are used to ease muscle and joint pains and inflammation. Also, warm or hot baths, with the addition of various substances such as seaweed extract to the water, may be used to help the healing of some skin conditions or minor wounds. After childbirth, frequent bathing in warm water to which a mild antiseptic has been added is recommended to heal skin tears.

Most people know the relaxing benefits of a hot bath. A bath with the temperature between 36.5°C and 40°C (98°F and 104°F) is very useful as a means of muscle relaxation. To begin with, five minutes immersion in a bath of this temperature is enough. This can be stepped up to ten minutes a day, as long as no feelings of weakness or dizziness arise. It is important to realize that a brief hot bath has quite a different effect from a long one.

There is nothing to be gained by prolonging a hot bath in the hope of increasing the benefit. Immersion in hot water acts not only on the surface nerves but also on the autonomic nervous system (which is normally outside our control), as well as the hormone-producing glands, particularly the adrenals, which become less active. A hot bath is sedative, but a hot bath that is prolonged into a long soak has quite the opposite effect.

Cold baths

Cold baths are used to improve blood flow to internal tissues and organs and to reduce swellings. The person may sit for a moment in shallow cold water with additional water being splashed onto exposed skin. An inflamed, painful part may be immersed in cold water to reduce swelling. The person is not allowed to become chilled, and this form of treatment is best suited for those able to dry themselves rapidly with a warm towel. It is not advisable for people with serious conditions or for the elderly or very young.

Neutral bath

There are many nerve endings on the skin surface and these deal with the reception of stimuli. More of these are cold receptors than heat receptors. If water of a different temperature from that of the skin is applied, it will either conduct heat to it or absorb heat from it. These stimuli have an influence on the sympathetic nervous system and can affect the hormonal system. The greater the difference between the temperature of the skin and the water applied, the greater will be the potential for physiological reaction. Conversely, water that is the same temperature as the body has a marked relaxing and sedative effect on the nervous system. This is of value in states of stress and has led to the development of the so-called 'neutral bath'.

Before the development of tranquillizers, the most dependable and effective method of calming an agitated patient was the use of a neutral bath. The patient was placed in a tub of water, the temperature of which was maintained at between 33.5°C and 35.6°C (92°F to 96°F), often for over three hours and sometimes for as long as twenty-four hours. Obviously, this is not a practical proposition for the average tense person.

As a self-help measure, the neutral bath does, however, offer a means of sedating the nervous system if used for relatively short periods. It is important to maintain the water temperature at the above level, and for this a bath thermometer should be used. The bathroom itself should be kept warm to prevent any chill in the air.

Half an hour of immersion in a bath like this will have a sedative, or even soporific, effect. It places no strain on the heart, circulation or nervous system and achieves muscular relaxation as well as a relaxation and expansion of the blood vessels: all these effects promote relaxation. This bath can be used in conjunction with other methods of relaxation, such as breathing techniques and meditation, to make it an even more efficient way of wiping out stress. It can be used daily if necessary.

Steam baths
Steam baths, along with saunas and Turkish baths, are used to encourage sweating and the opening of skin pores and have a cleansing and refreshing effect. The body may be able to eliminate harmful substances in this way, and treatment finishes with a cool bath.

Sitz baths
Sitz baths are usually given as a treatment for painful conditions with broken skin, such as piles or anal fissure, and also for ailments affecting the urinary and genital organs. The person sits in a specially designed bath that has two compartments, one with warm water, the other with cold. First, the person sits in the warm water, which covers the lower abdomen and hips, with the feet in the cold water compartment. After three minutes, the patient changes round and sits in the cold water with the feet in the warm compartment.

Hot and cold sprays
Hot and cold sprays of water may be given for a number of

different disorders but are not recommended for those with serious illnesses, elderly people or young children.

Wrapping

Wrapping is used for feverish conditions, backache and bronchitis. A cold wet sheet that has been squeezed out is wrapped
around the person, followed by a dry sheet and warm blanket.
These are left in place until the inner sheet has dried, and the
coverings are then removed. The body is sponged with tepid
water (at blood heat) before being dried with a towel. Sometimes the wrap is applied to a smaller area of the body, such as
the lower abdomen, to ease a particular problem, usually constipation.

Cold packs

Cold packs were described by the famous 19th-century Bavar-
ian pastor Sebastian Kniepp in his famous treatise *My Water
Cure*, in which he explained the advantages of hydrotherapy. A
cold pack is really a warm pack—the name comes from the
cold nature of the initial application.

For a cold pack you need: (1) a large piece of cotton material; (2) a large piece of flannel or woollen (blanket) material;
(3) a rubber sheet to protect the bed; (4) a hot-water bottle; (5)
safety pins.

First, soak the cotton material in very cold water, wring it out
well and place it on the flannel material that is spread out on
the rubber sheet on the bed. Lay the person who is having the
treatment on top of the damp material, fold it round his or her
trunk and cover him or her up at once with the flannel material.
Safety-pin it all firmly in place.

Now pull up the top bedcovers and provide a hot-water bottle. The initial cold application produces a reaction that draws
fresh blood to the surface of the body; this warmth, being well

insulated, is retained by the damp material. The cold pack turns into a warm pack, which gradually, over a period of six to eight hours, bakes itself dry. Usually lots of sweat will be produced, so it is necessary to wash the materials well before using again.

The pack can be slept in—in fact it should encourage deeper, more refreshing sleep. Larger, whole-body packs can be used, which cover not only the trunk but extend from the armpits to the feet, encasing the recipient in a cocoon of warmth.

If a feeling of damp coldness is felt, the wet material may be inadequately wrung out or the insulation materials too loose or too few.

Flotation

A form of sensory deprivation, flotation involves lying face up in an enclosed, dark tank of warm, heavily salted water. There is no sound, except perhaps some natural music to bring the client into a dream-like state. It is exceptionally refreshing and induces a deep, relaxing sleep.

Kinesiology

The function of kinesiology

Kinesiology is a method of maintaining health by ensuring that all muscles are functioning correctly. It is believed that each muscle is connected with a specific part of the body, such as the digestive system, circulation of the blood and specific organs, and that if a muscle is not functioning correctly this will cause a problem in its related part of the body. The word is derived from *kinesis*, which is Greek for 'motion'. Kinesiology originated in 1964 and was developed by an American chiropractor named George Goodheart who realized that while he was treating a patient for severe pain in the leg, by massaging a particular muscle in the upper leg, the pain experienced by the patient eased and the muscle was strengthened. Although he used the same method on different muscles, the results were not the same. Previous research done by an osteopath named Dr Chapman, in the 1900s, indicated that there were certain 'pressure points' in the body that were connected with particular muscles and, if these were massaged, lymph would be able to flow more freely through the body. Using these pressure points, Chapman found which point was connected to each particular muscle and realized why, when he had massaged a patient's upper leg muscle, the pain had lessened. The pressure point for that leg muscle was the only one that was situated above the actual muscle—all the other points were not close to the part of the body with which they were connected.

The use of pressure points

In the 1930s it was claimed that there were similar pressure points located on the skull and that, by exerting a light pressure on these, the flow of blood to their related organs could be assisted. Goodheart tested this claim, which originated from an osteopath called Terence Bennett, and discovered that after only fingertip pressure for a matter of seconds, the strength of a particular muscle was improved. After some time he was able to locate sixteen points on the head, the back of the knee and by the breastbone that were all allied to groups of important muscles. Goodheart was surprised that so little force applied on the pressure point could have such an effect on the muscle, so to further his studies he then applied himself to acupuncture, the form of healing that also makes use of certain points located over the body but running along specific paths known as *meridians*. After further study, Goodheart came to the conclusion that the meridians could be used for both muscles and organs. The invisible paths used in kinesiology are exactly the same as the ones for acupuncture.

Energy and lymph

A kinesiologist will examine a patient to try to discover whether there is any lack of energy, physical disorders or inadequate nutrition that are causing problems. Once any troublesome areas have been located, the practitioner will use only a light massage on the relevant pressure points (which, as mentioned, are generally not close to their associated muscle). For example, the edge of the rib cage is where the pressure points for the muscles of the upper leg are situated. In kinesiology it is maintained that the use of pressure points is effective because the flow of blood to muscles is stimulated and therefore a good supply of lymph is generated too. Lymph is a watery fluid that takes toxins from the tissues, and if muscles receive a good supply of both lymph and blood they should function efficiently. As in acupuncture, it is maintained that there is an unseen flow of energy that runs through the body. If this is disrupted for any reason, such as a person being ill or suffering from stress, then the body will weaken as a result of the insufficient energy being produced. The way in which a kinesiologist assesses the general health of a patient is by testing the strength of the muscles as this will provide information on the flow of energy. It is claimed that by finding any inbalance and correcting it, kinesiology can be used as a preventative therapy. If there is a lack of minerals and vitamins in the body or trouble with the digestive system, it is claimed that these can be diagnosed by the use of kinesiology. If a person is feeling 'below par' and constantly feels tired, it is believed that this condition is aggravated by a sluggish flow of the internal body fluids, such as the circulation of blood. Kinesiologists can treat the disorder by stimulating the flow of lymph and blood by massaging the pressure points.

Although it is claimed that kinesiology can be of help to all people, it is widely known for the treatment of people suffering from food allergies or those who are sensitive to some foods. It is believed that the chemicals and nutrients contained in food cause various reactions in the body, and if a particular food has the effect of making muscles weak, then it would be concluded that a person has an allergy to it. Allergic reactions can cause other problems such as headaches, tension, colds, tiredness and a general susceptibility to acquiring any passing infections.

There are two simple tests that can easily be tried at home to determine if there is any sensitivity or allergy to certain foods. This is done by testing the strength of a strong muscle in the chest, and to carry this out the person being tested will need the help of a partner. There is no need to exert real force at any time, just use the minimum amount needed to be firm but gentle. To test the chest muscle, sit erect, holding the left arm straight out at right angles to the body. The elbow should be facing outwards and the fingers and thumb drooping towards the table. The partner then places his or her right hand on the person's nearest shoulder (the right) and the two fingers only on the area around the left wrist. A gentle downward pressure is then exerted by the partner on the person's wrist. The person then tries to maintain the level of the arm while breathing in a normal fashion. This downward pressure should be exerted for approximately five seconds. If the person was able to resist the downwards pressure and the muscle felt quite firm, then the allergy test can be tried. If this was not the case, however, and the person was unable to keep the arm level, the muscle would not be suitable for use in the subsequent test. It would therefore be advisable to use another muscle, such as one in the arm. To do this, place an arm straight down at the side of the body with the palm of the hands facing outwards. The partner then uses the same amount of pressure to try to move the arm outwards, again for a similar amount of time. If the person is unable to keep the arm in the same position, then it would be advisable to get in touch with a trained kinesiologist.

To undertake the allergy test, hold the left arm in the same way as for testing the muscle (*see* page 50, figure A). If, for example, the food that is suspected of causing an allergy is chocolate, a small piece of this should be put just in the mouth; there is no need for it to be eaten. This time, as well as applying the pressure on the wrist as before, the partner should put his or her first two digits of the left hand below the person's right ear. Once again, the person tries to resist the downwards force and, if successful, it is claimed that there is no sensitivity or allergy

Figure A—determining sensitivity or allergy to foods

connected with that food. However, if this does not happen and the arm is pushed downwards or even feels slightly weak, then kinesiology would suggest that this food, if eaten at all, should never be consumed in any great amount.

It is claimed that the use of kinesiology can be of benefit to people who suffer from irrational fears or phobias. An example of this is the recommendation that the bone below the eye, just in line with the pupil, is softly tapped.

Neck and back pain can be treated without any manipulation of joints, and some of the methods can be learnt by patients for use at home. An example of this, for the alleviation of back pain, is for a patient to massage the muscle situated on the inside of the thigh. This is said to be of benefit for any muscles that are weak as they are one reason for a painful back.

A number of other practitioners, such as homeopaths, herbalists and osteopaths, make use of kinesiology, so if there is a problem connected with the ligaments, muscles or bones it may be advisable to contact a chiropractor or osteopath who is also qualified in kinesiology. If the problem is of a more emotional or mental nature, then it might be best to select a counsellor or psychotherapist who also practises kinesiology. It is important always to use a fully qualified practitioner, and the relevant association should be contacted for information. At the first consultation, detailed questions will be asked concerning the medical history, followed by the therapist checking the muscles' ability to function effectively. For instance, a slight pressure will be exerted on a leg or arm while the patient holds it in a certain way. The patient's ability to maintain that position against the pressure is noted, and if the patient is unable to do this, then the therapist will find the reason why by further examination. Once the areas in need of 'rebalancing' have been identified, the therapist will use the relevant pressure points to correct matters. It is believed that if some of the points are painful or sore to the touch, this is because there has been an accumulation of toxins in the tissues and that these toxins stop the impulses between muscles and the brain. If this is the case, the muscle is unable to relax properly and can cause problems in areas such as the neck and shoulders.

There are ways of identifying any possible problems. For example, if there is any weakness in the shoulder muscle it may be that there is some problem connected with the lungs. To test for this, the patient sits upright with one arm raised to slightly below shoulder level and the other arm lower and out to the front. The therapist grasps the patient's upper arm and presses gently downwards on the raised arm at the elbow (*see* page 52, figure B). If the muscle is functioning correctly then

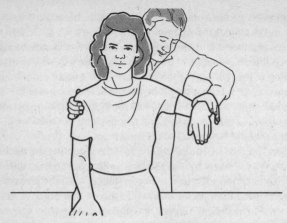

Figure B—determining whether there is weakness in the shoulder muscle

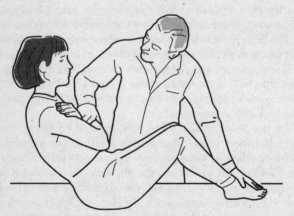

Figure C—determining whether there are weak muscles in the stomach

this downwards force should not be allowed to move the arm lower. If the patient is suffering from pain in the back, the probable cause lies with weak muscles in the stomach. To test for this, the patient sits on the floor with the knees raised, the arms crossed on the chest and then he or she leans backwards (*see* page 52 figure C). The therapist checks the stomach muscles' efficiency by pushing gently backwards on the patient's crossed arms. If all is well the patient should be able to maintain the position and not lean back any further.

After treatment by massage of the pressure points, there may well be some tenderness experienced for one or two days as the toxins in the tissues gradually dissipate. However, there should be an overall feeling of an improvement in health and in particular with the problem that was being treated.

Although there has been an increase in the use of kinesiology by doctors to help discover the cause of an ailment, there has been little scientific research carried out. The majority of doctors using conventional medicine therefore do not believe that the flow of electrical energy present in the body can be changed by the use of massage or similar methods.

Massage

Introduction

Origins

We massage ourselves nearly every day. The natural reaction
to reach out and touch a painful part of the body—such as a
sprain—forms the basis of massage. As long ago as 3000 BC
massage was used as a therapy in the Far East, making it one of
the oldest treatments used by humans. In 5 BC in ancient Greece,
Hippocrates recommended that to maintain health, a massage
using oils should be taken daily after a perfumed bath. Greek
physicians were well used to treating people who suffered from
pain and stiffness in the joints. The relaxation and healing powers of massage have been well documented over the past 5,000
years.

The therapeutic value of applying oils and rubbing parts of
the body to lessen pain and prevent illness was recognized
among the ancient Mediterranean civilizations. In ancient times
scented oils were almost always used when giving massages,
creating an early form of aromatherapy massage.

Popularity

Massage increased in popularity when, in the 19th century, Per
Henrik Ling, a Swedish fencing master and academic, created
the basis for what is now known as Swedish massage. Swedish
massage deals with the soft tissues of the body.

Swedish massage is a combination of relaxing effects and
exercises that work on the joints and muscles, but it is still based

on the form that was practised in ancient times. More recently, a work was published in the 1970s called *The Massage Book,* by George Downing, and this introduced a new concept in the overall technique of massage, that the whole person's state should be assessed by the therapist and not solely the physical side. The emotional and mental states should be part of the overall picture. Also combined in his form of massage were the methods used in reflexology (*see* page 94) and shiatsu (*see* page 171), and this was known as therapeutic massage. The aim of this is to use relaxation, stimulation and invigoration to promote good health.

Uses

Massage is commonly used to induce general relaxation so that any tension or strain experienced in the rush of daily life can be eased and eliminated. It is found to be very effective, working on the mind as well as the body. It can be used to treat people with hypertension (high blood pressure), sinusitis, headaches, insomnia and hyperactivity, including people who suffer from heart ailments or circulatory disorders. At the physical level, massage is intended to help the body make use of food and to eliminate the waste materials, as well as stimulating the nervous and muscular system and the circulation of blood. Neck and back pain are conditions from which many people suffer, particularly if they have not been sitting correctly, such as in a slightly stooped position with their shoulders rounded. People whose day-to-day work involves a great deal of physical activity, such as dancers and athletes, can also derive a great deal of benefit from the use of massage. Stiffness can be a problem that they have after training or working, and this is relieved by encouraging the toxins that gather in the muscles to disperse. Massage promotes a feeling of calmness and serenity, and this is particularly beneficial to people who frequently suffer from bouts of depression or anxiety. Once the worry and depression have been dispelled, people are able to deal with their problems much more effectively and, being able to do so, will boost their self-confidence.

Medical use

An aid to recovery

In hospitals, massage has been used to ease pain and discomfort as well as being of benefit to people who are bedridden, since the flow of blood to the muscles is stimulated. It has also been used for those who have suffered a heart attack and has helped their recovery. A more recent development has been the use of massage for cancer patients who are suffering from the after-effects of treatment, such as chemotherapy, as well as the discomfort the disease itself causes. Indeed, there are few conditions when it is not recommended. However, it should not be used when people are suffering from inflammation of the veins (phlebitis), varicose veins, thrombosis (clots in the blood) or if they have a raised temperature such as occurs during a fever. It is then advisable to contact a doctor before using massage. Doctors may be able to recommend a qualified therapist, a health centre may be able to help or contact can be made with the relevant professional body.

Psychological benefits

Along with the diagnosis element of massage there are great psychological benefits—the enjoyment of touch and of being stroked and caressed by another person. During a massage the patient is coaxed from emotional and occupational stresses and brought into the intense arena of the here and now. The importance of this kind of one-on-one nonverbal communication can never be underestimated in our increasingly impersonal and detached society.

Massage has a wide range of uses for a variety of disorders. Its strengths lie in the easing of strain and tension and inducing relaxation and serenity, plus the physical contact of the therapist. Although doctors make use of this therapy in conjunction with orthodox medicine, it is not to be regarded as a cure for diseases in itself and serious problems could occur if this were the case.

Benefits

Massage affects the whole body through rhythmically applied pressure. Gentle pulling and stroking movements increase the circulation of the blood and cause the blood vessels to dilate. The stimulation of nerves and blood will also affect the internal organs. Lymph is a milky white liquid that carries waste substances and toxins away from the tissues via the lymphatic system. Inactivity can cause an unhealthy build-up of this substance, and as the circulation of the lymph is largely dependent on muscle contractions, so massage will help speed the lymph's progress through the system. Active people can also benefit from massage as strenuous activity burns up the muscle, producing an increase of waste products in the muscle tissue. Massage will help to balance the system in both cases and can increase oxygen capacity by 10–15 per cent.

Massage can go a long way to repairing our damaged postures. Inactive lifestyles and sedentary occupations have created a society of people with cramped, stooped and neglected postures. Not only does massage help to coax the spine and corresponding physiology back into position, it also makes us more aware of our bodies. Relieved of muscle tension, the body feels lighter and can therefore be borne more naturally and with more poise. Used in conjunction with postural therapies such as Pilates or the Alexander technique (*see* page 15), massage can help achieve a relaxed yet controlled posture.

Women in labour have found that the pain experienced during childbirth can be eased if massage is performed on the buttocks and back. The massage eases the build-up of tension in the muscles, encouraging relaxation and easing of labour pains. It is said to be more effective on women who had previously experienced the benefits and reassurance of massage.

Many of the benefits of massage come through the healer/patient contact. Our hands are one of the most sensitive parts of our body, and we experience much of our sense of touch through our hands. An experienced masseur or masseuse is able to use his or her hands to communicate feelings of harmony and relaxation. A practised masseur will also be able to diagnose the patient through touch. He or she can 'listen' to tension and stress through the texture of the skin, knotted muscles and stiff joints. Old and current sprains, congestion and swelling should all be obvious to a good masseur. The actions of massage—the stroking, kneading and pulling—detoxify the body, improving circulation and lymphatic drainage. After tension and weaknesses in the body have been pinpointed and relieved, the patient is left feeling relaxed and energized.

The massage session

Preparation

A session may be undertaken in the patient's home, or he or she can attend the masseur at a clinic. At each session the client will undress, leaving only pants or briefs on, and will lie on a firm, comfortable surface, such as a table that is designed especially for massage. The massage that follows normally lasts from 20 minutes to one hour.

If performed by professionals, massage is not a technique for the unduly modest. It achieves best results if the person receiving the massage is either naked or else dressed in the scantiest of underwear. For anyone who is competent and wishes to provide some simple massage for a partner, there are some basic rules to follow. The room should be warm and peaceful. The surface on which the person lies should be quite comfortable but firm. Use a mid-thigh-level table or the floor. A futon (a quilted Japanese mattress) can be used, and to relieve the upper part of the body from any possible discomfort, a pillow should be placed underneath the torso. Any pressure that may be exerted on the feet can be dispelled by the use of a rolled-up towel or similar placed beneath the ankles. Both people should be relaxed, and to this end soft music can be played. All the movements of the hand should be of a continuous nature. It is suggested that the recipient always has one hand of the masseur placed on him or her. If you wish you can buy a perfumed massage oil from a pharmacy or health shop, or mix your own using a blend of aromatherapy oils. Vegetable oil (about one teaspoonful) is suitable but should not be poured straight on to the person. It should be spread over the hands by rubbing, which will also warm it sufficiently for use. Should the masseur get out of breath, he or she should stop for a rest, all the while retaining a hand on the person.

Basic techniques

Massage can be divided into four basic forms, and these are known as *percussion* (also known as drumming); *friction* (also called pressure); *effleurage* (also called stroking) and *petrissage* (also called kneading). These methods can be practised alone or in combination for maximum benefit to the patient.

Percussion (drumming or tapotement)

Percussion is also called tapotement, which is derived from *tapoter*, a French word that means 'to drum', as of the fingers on a surface. As would be expected from its name, percussion is generally done with the edge of the hand with a quick, chopping movement, although the strokes are not hard. This type of movement would be used on places like the buttocks, thighs, waist or shoulders where there is a wide expanse of flesh.

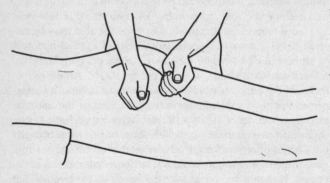

Percussion

Friction (pressure)

Friction strokes are used to penetrate into deep muscle tissue. Friction is often used on dancers and athletes who experience problems with damaged ligaments or tendons. This is because the flow of blood is stimulated and the movement of joints is improved. Friction can be performed with the base of the hand, some fingers or the upper part of the thumb. It is not advisable to use this method on parts of the body that have been injured in some way, for example where there is bruising.

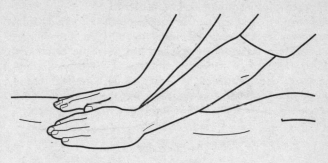

Friction

Effleurage (stroking)

Effleurage is performed in a slow, rhythmical, controlled manner using both hands together with a small space between the thumbs (A). If the therapist wishes to use only light pressure he or she will use the palms of the hands or the tips of the fingers with light gliding strokes, working away from the heart. Light gliding strokes have a relaxing effect on the nervous system. For increased pressure the knuckles or thumbs will be used in an upwards stroking motion towards the heart. Stronger pressure has more of an effect on the blood circulation and the nervous system.

Effleurage can be used on the upper leg as far up as the hip on the outside of the leg. Once the person is lying face downwards (with support under the chest), continue to use effleurage movements on the back of the lower leg. Continue as before but work on the upper leg (B), avoiding the knee. The muscles in the buttocks can be worked upon with both hands to squeeze but making sure that the hands are moving in opposite ways (C).

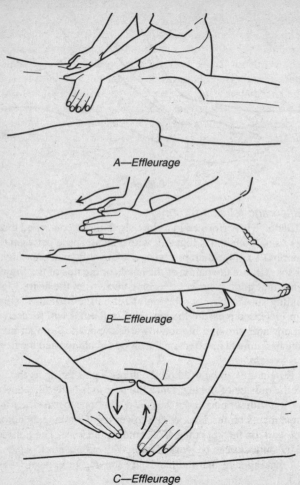

A—Effleurage

B—Effleurage

C—Effleurage

Petrissage (kneading)

Petrissage is ideal for unlocking aching or tense muscles, in particular the trapezium muscle between the neck and shoulders (A). Both hands work together in a rhythmic sequence, alternately picking up and gently squeezing the tense muscle. The kneading action gets deep enough to stimulate the lymph into removing the build-up of lactic acid. As the therapist works across each section, an area of flesh is grasped and squeezed, and this action stimulates the flow of blood and enables tensed muscles to relax. People such as athletes can have an accumu-

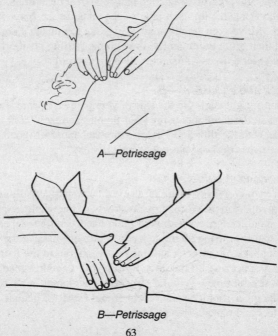

A—Petrissage

B—Petrissage

lation of lactic acid in certain muscles, and this is why cramp occurs. Parts of the body on which this method is practised are along the stomach and around the waist (B).

Neck and shoulder massage

What follows can be used to relieve headaches, loosen the shoulder muscles and provide a general feeling of relaxation.

Neck and shoulders—A

Stand behind your seated partner. Begin with effleurage, applying firm pressure with both hands. Start at the bottom of the shoulder blades up each side of the spine to the base of the neck. Move your hands apart across the top of the shoulders and then bring them gently down to the starting position. Repeat several times, finishing with a light return stroke.

Neck and shoulders—B

Stand at right angles to the side of your partner. Locate tension spots in the shoulders using your thumbs and then work these areas with the thumbs. The pressure can approach your partner's pain threshold but not exceed it.

Neck and shoulders—C

Place your left hand in an 'L' shape on your partner's shoulder. Applying firm pressure, move it slowly up the whole length of the shoulder. Repeat with your other hand. Continue repeating the sequence using alternate hands. Place one hand at the base of the back of the neck and move it gently up to the hairline, gently squeezing all the time. Return with a gentle stroke. Repeat several times. Without removing your hands, walk round to the other shoulder and repeat B and C. Move behind your partner and repeat A several times.

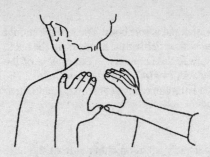

A—Neck and shoulders

B—Neck and shoulders

C—Neck and shoulders

Back massage

Back massage helps to relax the whole body. The strokes should be carried out smoothly, without lifting the hands from the back. Applying thumb pressure to the channels on either side of the spine on the upper back will help respiratory problems. The same stroke on the lower back can relieve constipation and menstrual discomfort.

Back—A

Place your hands, facing each other, on either side of the base of the spine. Move them up the back, using your body weight to apply pressure. Take your hands round the shoulders and return lightly down the sides of the body. Repeat several times before stopping to knead the shoulders. Work on one shoulder and then the other. Repeat the movement.

Back—B

Place your hands at waist level, with your thumbs in the hollows on either side of the spine and your fingers open and relaxed. Push your thumbs firmly up the channels for about 6 cm (2 in), relax them, and then move them back about 2 cm (1 in). Continue in this way up to the neck. Then gently slide both hands back to the base of the spine. Repeat. Follow with the sequence in A.

Back—C

Place your hand flat across one side of your partner's back at the base of the spine. Apply firm palm pressure and work up to the shoulders. Follow closely with your other hand. Repeat using alternate hands. Work through the same sequence on the other side of the back, then repeat on both side several times. Finish by working through A.

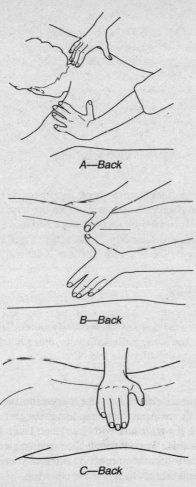

A—Back

B—Back

C—Back

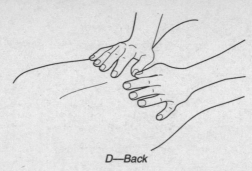

D—Back

Back—D
Place your hands, facing up the back, on either side of the spine.
Applying firm palm pressure, work from the base of the spine
to chest level. Turn your fingers outwards and move your hands
apart to the sides of the body. Repeat this stroke at waist and
hip levels. Repeat the first movement in A several times.

Limb massage

Limbs—A
Begin at the ankle and stroke vertically up the leg with one
hand. Follow the same path with your other hand. Continue
this sequence, using alternate hands.

Limbs—B
Raise your partner's foot and hold it with the knee at a right
angle. Using the palm of your free hand, stroke firmly down
the back of the leg from ankle to knee level. Use a light stroke
to return to the ankle. Repeat the whole movement several times.
If including the foot, work through D and E next before repeating the full sequence (A to B) on the other leg.

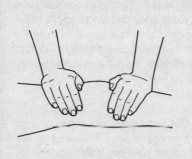

A—Limbs

B—Limbs

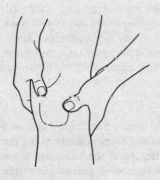

C—Limbs

D—Limbs

Alternative Therapies

Limbs—C

Help your partner to turn over, and begin by stroking with alternate hands up the whole leg, as in A. Then put your hands on either side of the knee and, using your thumbs to apply pressure, circle around the knee cap. If including the foot, bring your hands down to the ankle and use the sandwich stroke (D) on the front of the foot. Work through the full movement on the other leg.

Limbs—D

With your partner lying face down, take one foot between your hands, so that the palm of your upper hand is resting in the arch. Press firmly, and slowly draw your hands down to the tip of the foot. Use plenty of pressure for this 'sandwich' stoke.

Limbs—E

Hold the foot with your thumbs lying side by side behind the toes. Pull both thumbs back to the sides of the foot, then push them forward. Repeat this zig-zag movement as you work down to the heel. Then push firmly all the way back to the toes, keeping your thumbs side by side. Repeat the whole movement several times. Work through the whole sequence (D to E) on the other foot.

Limbs—F

Take hold of your partner's hand as in a firm handshake, and lift the arm up slightly, as far as the elbow. Gently place the palm of your free hand across the top of the wrist and close your fingers round the raised arm. Apply firm pressure and slide your hand up to the elbow or as far as the shoulder. Move your palm underneath the arm and use a light stroke to return to the wrist. Repeat several times.

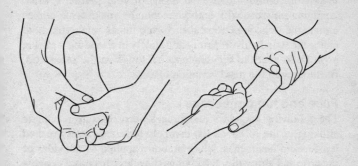

E—Limbs   *F—Limbs*

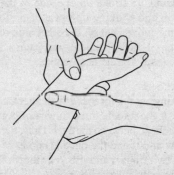

G—Limbs

Limbs—G

Place your thumbs across the inside of your partner's wrist. Applying pressure with both your thumbs, make wide circles around the wrist area. Repeat F. As you finish, relax your hold on the wrist and pull off firmly and slowly in a sandwich stroke, as in D. Repeat the full sequence (F to G) on the other arm, finishing with the hand variation of D.

Face and head massage

The following sequence encourages deep relaxation. Gentle stroking of the forehead (B) can help to relieve stress-related tension and headaches, while pressure applied to the sides of the nose and along the cheekbones (C) alleviates nasal congestion and sinus problems. Scalp massage (D) stimulates circulation.

Face and head—A

Use alternate hands to stroke up one side of the face, starting beneath the chin and working up towards the forehead. Work through the same movement on the other side of the face. Repeat several times. Finish by placing one palm across your partner's forehead, ready for the next stroke.

Face and head—B

Begin by stroking up the forehead with alternate palms. Then place the pads of the middle three fingers of both hands in the centre of the forehead between the eyes. Draw them gently apart across the brow and round the outside corner of the eyes. Lift off the middle two fingers and use your fourth fingers only to return under the eyes towards the nose.

Face and head—C

Position your thumbs on your partner's forehead. Using the

three middle fingers of both hands, press firmly against the sides of the nose. Continue along the top of the cheekbone until you reach the temple. Keeping your thumbs in position, return to the nose, pressing along the middle of the cheekbone.

Face and head—D
Spread out the fingers and thumbs of both hands and place them on your partner's scalp. Keep them in position and begin to move the scalp muscle over the bone by applying gentle pressure and circling slowly and firmly on the spot. Stop occasionally to move to a different area, then begin again, working gradually over the whole scalp.

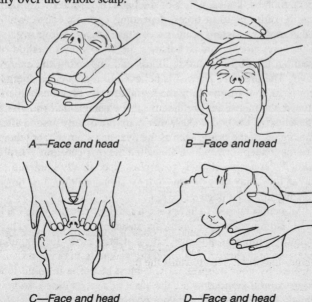

A—Face and head

B—Face and head

C—Face and head

D—Face and head

73

Acupressure

This is an ancient form of healing combining massage and acupuncture, practised over 3,000 years ago in Japan and China. It was developed into its current form using a system of special massage points and is today still practised widely in the Japanese home environment.

Certain 'pressure points' are located in various parts of the body, and these are used by the acupressurist by massaging firmly with the thumb or fingertip. These points are the same as those utilized in acupuncture. There are various ways of working and the pressure can be applied by the acupressurist's fingers, thumbs, knees, palms of the hand, etc. Relief from pain can be quite rapid at times, depending upon its cause, while other more persistent problems can take longer to improve.

Acupressure is said to enhance the body's own method of healing, thereby preventing illness and improving the energy level. The pressure exerted is believed to regulate the energy, chi or qi, that flows along the meridians. As previously mentioned, the meridians are the invisible channels that run along the length of the body. These meridians are mainly named after the organs of the body, such as the liver and stomach, but there are four exceptions, which are called the 'pericardium', 'triple heater', 'conception' and 'governor'. Specifically named meridian lines may also be used to treat ailments other than those relating to it (*see* page 9).

Ailments claimed to have been treated successfully are back pain, asthma, digestive problems, insomnia, migraine and circulatory problems amongst others. Changes in diet, regular exercise and certain self-checking methods may be recommended by your acupressurist. It must be borne in mind that some painful symptoms are the onset of serious illness so you should always first consult your doctor.

Before any treatment commences, a patient will be asked details of lifestyle and diet and the pulse rate will be taken along with any relevant past history relating to the current problem. The person will be requested to lie on a mattress on the floor or on a firm table, and comfortable but loose-fitting clothing is best so that the acupressurist can work most effectively on the energy channels. No oils are used on the body and there is no equipment. Each session lasts from approximately 30 minutes to one hour. Once the pressure is applied, and this can be done in a variety of ways particular to each acupressurist, varying sensations may be felt. Some points may feel sore or tender and there may be some discomfort, such as a deep pain or coolness. However, it is believed that this form of massage works quickly so that any tenderness soon passes.

The number of treatments will vary from patient to patient, according to how the person responds and what problem or ailment is being treated. Weekly visits may be needed if a specific disorder is being treated while other people may go whenever they feel in need. It is advisable for women who are pregnant to check with their doctor first since some of the acupressure methods are not recommended during pregnancy. Acupressure can be practised safely at home although it is usually better for one person to perform the massage on another. Common problems such as headache, constipation and toothache can be treated quite simply, although there is the possibility of a problem worsening first before an improvement occurs if the pressure points are over-stimulated. You should, however, see your doctor if any ailment persists. To treat headache, facial soreness, toothache and menstrual pain, locate the fleshy piece of skin between the thumb and forefinger and squeeze firmly, pressing towards the forefinger. The pressure should be applied for about five minutes and either hand can be used. This point is known as 'large intestine 4'.

To aid digestive problems in both adults and babies, for example to settle infantile colic, the point known as 'stomach 36' is utilized, which is located on the outer side of the leg about 75mm (3 ins) down from the knee. This point should be quite simple to find as it can often feel slightly tender. It should be pressed quite firmly and strongly for about five to ten minutes with the thumb.

When practising acupressure massage on someone else and before treatment begins, ensure that the person is warm, relaxed, comfortable and wearing loose-fitting clothing and that he or she is lying on a firm mattress or rug on the floor. To discover the areas that need to be worked on, press firmly over the body and see which areas are tender. These tender areas on

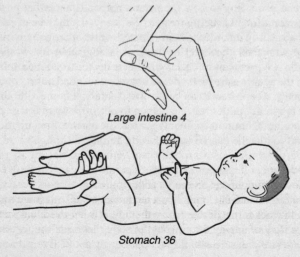

Large intestine 4

Stomach 36

the body correspond to an organ that is not working correctly. To commence massage using fingertips or thumbs, a pressure of about 4.5 kg (10 lbs) should be exerted. The massage movements should be performed very quickly, about 50 to 100 times every minute, and some discomfort is likely (which will soon pass) but there should be no pain. Particular care should be taken to avoid causing pain on the face, stomach or over any joints. If a baby or young child is being massaged then considerably less pressure should be used. If there is any doubt as to the correct amount, exert a downwards pressure on bathroom scales to ascertain the weight being used. There is no need to hurry from one point to another since approximately 5 to 15 minutes is needed at each point for adults, but only about 30 seconds for babies or young children.

Using 'self-help' acupressure, massage can be repeated as often as is felt to be necessary, with several sessions per hour usually being sufficient for painful conditions that have arisen suddenly. It is possible that as many as 20 sessions may be necessary for persistent conditions causing pain, with greater intervals of time between treatments as matters improve. It is not advisable to try anything that is at all complicated (or to treat an illness such as arthritis) and a trained practitioner will obviously be able to provide the best level of treatment and help. To contact a reputable practitioner who has completed the relevant training it is advisable to contact the appropriate professional body.

Do-in

Do-in (pronounced doe-in) is another ancient type of massage that originated in China. It is a technique of self-massage and, as in other forms of alternative therapy, it is believed that there is a flow of energy throughout the body that travels along *meridians* and that each of these is connected to a vital organ such as the lungs, liver and heart. Do-in has a connection with shiatsu (*see* page 171), and people of any age can participate, the only stipulation being that they are active and not out of condition. Clothing should not be tight or restrictive and adequate space is needed to perform the exercises.

If do-in is to be used as an invigorating form of massage, then the best time of day is as soon as possible after rising but not after breakfast. After meals are the only times when do-in is to be avoided. It is generally recommended that people wishing to practise do-in should first go to classes so that when the exercises are done at home they are performed correctly. It is claimed that the use of do-in is preventative in nature since the vital organs are strengthened and therefore maintained in a healthy state.

Warming up

Before starting, it is best to do some warming-up exercises so that the body is not stiff. Begin by sitting on the ground with the knees up, grasp the knees and begin a rocking motion forwards and backwards. Then sit up, again on the floor, position the legs as if to sit cross-legged but put the soles of the feet touching each other. Hold the toes for a short time. These two exercises should help to make the body more supple (A).

A—warming up

B—spleen meridian   C—bladder meridian

Spleen meridian

For the spleen meridian exercise, which is connected with the stomach, stand as near as possible in front of a wall. Place one hand palm-downwards high up the wall so that there is a good stretching action and with the other hand grasp the foot that is opposite to the raised arm. The neck and head should be stretched backwards, away from the wall. Maintain this stretched position, inhale and exhale deeply twice and then relax. Repeat the procedure using the other arm and leg (B).

Bladder meridian

For the bladder meridian exercise, and thereby the kidneys, sit on the floor with the legs straight out in front and ensure that the toes are tensed upright. The arms should then be stretched above the head and a breath taken. After breathing out, bend forwards from the shoulders with the arms in front and hold the toes. Maintain this for the length of time it takes to breathe in and out three times. Repeat the procedure again (C).

Pericardium meridian

To do the exercise for the pericardium meridian, which affects the circulation, sit on the floor with feet touching, but one behind the other, ensuring that the hands are crossed and touching opposite knees. Grasp the knees and incline the body forwards with the aim of pushing the knees downwards on to the floor. Do this exercise again but with the hands on opposite knees and the other foot on the outside.

Large intestine meridian

To use the exercise that strengthens the large intestine meridian, and in turn the lungs, stand upright with the feet apart. Link the thumbs behind the back and then inhale. Exhale and at the same time place the arms outwards and upwards behind the

D—Large intestine meridian

back. To complete the exercise, lean forwards from the hips and then stand upright (D).

Gall bladder meridian

To strengthen the liver by stimulating the gall bladder meridian, sit upright on the floor with the legs the maximum distance apart. Then inhale, passing the arms along the length of the right leg so that the base of the foot can be held. There should be no movement of the buttocks off the floor. Maintain this stretched position while breathing deeply twice. Repeat the exercise using the other leg

After all exercises have been accomplished, lie flat out on the floor with the legs apart and the arms stretched at the sides, palms uppermost. Then lift the head so that the feet can be seen and then put the head back on the floor again. The head and body should then be shaken so that the legs, arms and neck are loosened. To complete the relaxation, the eyes should be closed and the person should lie quietly for a few minutes.

Osteopathy

Introduction

An alternative medical treatment

Osteopathy is a technique that uses manipulation and massage to help distressed muscles and joints and make them work smoothly.

The profession began in 1892 when Dr Andrew Taylor Still (1828–1917), an American farmer, inventor and doctor, opened the USA's first school of osteopathic medicine. He sought alternatives to the medical treatments of his day, which he believed were ineffective as well as often harmful.

Still's new philosophy of medicine, based upon the teachings of Hippocrates, advocated that 'Finding health should be the purpose of a doctor. Anyone can find disease.' Like Hippocrates, Still recognized that the human body is a unit in which structure, function, mind and spirit all work together. The therapy aims to pinpoint and treat any problems that are of a mechanical nature. The body's frame consists of the skeleton, muscles, joints and ligaments, and all movements or activities, such as running, swimming, eating, speaking and walking, depend upon it.

A holistic treatment

Still came to believe that it would be safer to encourage the body to heal itself rather than use the drugs that were then available and that were not always safe. He regarded the body from an engineer's point of view, and the combination of this and his medical experience of anatomy led him to believe that ailments and disorders could occur when the bones or joints no longer functioned in harmony. He believed that manipulation was the cure for the problem. Although his ideas provoked a great deal of opposition from the American medical profession at first, they slowly came to be accepted. The bulk of scientific research has been done in America, with a number of medical schools of osteopathy being established. Dr Martin Littlejohn, who was a pupil of Dr Still, brought the practice of osteopathy to the United Kingdom around 1900, with the first school being founded in 1917 in London. He emphasized the compassionate care and treatment of the person as a whole, not as a collection of symptoms or unrelated parts. The philosophy and practices of Dr Still, considered radical in the late 19th and early 20th centuries, are generally accepted principles of good medicine today.

Injuries and stress

Problems that prevent the body from working correctly or that create pain can be caused by injury or stress. The result can be known as a tension headache since the stress experienced causes a contraction in muscles. These muscles are situated at the back of the neck at the base of the skull, and relief can be obtained by the use of massage. In osteopathy, it is believed that if the basic framework of the body is undamaged, then all physical activities can be accomplished efficiently and without causing any problems. The majority of an osteopath's patients suffer from disorders of the spine, which result in pain in the lower part of the back and the neck. A great deal of pressure is exerted on the spinal column and especially on the cartilage between the individual vertebrae. Because of the effects of gravity this is a constant pressure that occurs merely by standing. If a person stands incorrectly, with stooped shoulders, this will exacerbate any problems or perhaps initiate one. The joints and framework of the body are manipulated and massaged where necessary so that the usual action is regained.

Athletes or dancers can receive injuries to muscles or joints such as the ankle, hip, wrist or elbow, and they too can benefit from treatment by osteopathy. Pain in the lower back can be experienced by pregnant women who may stand in a different way because of their increasing weight, and if this is the case osteopathy can often ease matters considerably. To find a fully qualified osteopath, it is advisable to contact the relevant professional body, or your doctor may be able to help.

The treatment

The first visit
At the first visit to an osteopath, he or she will need to learn the complete history of any problems experienced, how they first occurred and what eases or aggravates matters. A patient's case history and any form of therapy that is currently in use will all be of relevance to the practitioner. A thorough examination will then take place, observing how the patient sits, stands or lies down and also the manner in which the body is bent to the side, back or front. As each movement takes place, the osteopath is able to take note of the extent and ability of the joint to function. The practitioner will also feel the muscles, soft tissues and ligaments to detect if there is any tension present. Whilst examining the body, the osteopath will note any problems that are present and, as an aid to diagnosis, use may also be made of checking reflexes, such as the knee-jerk reflex. If a patient has been involved in an accident, X-rays can be checked to determine the extent of any problem. It is possible that a disorder would not benefit from treatment by osteopathy and the patient

would be advised accordingly. If this is not the case, treatment can commence with the chosen course of therapy.

A solution to tension

There is no set number of consultations necessary, as this will depend upon the nature of the problem and also for how long it has been apparent. It is possible that a severe disorder that has arisen suddenly can be alleviated at once. The osteopath is likely to recommend a number of things so that patients can help themselves between treatments. Techniques such as learning to relax, how to stand and sit correctly and additional exercises can be suggested by the osteopath. Patients generally find that each consultation is quite pleasant and they feel much more relaxed and calm afterwards. The length of each session can vary, but it is generally in the region of half an hour. As the osteopath gently manipulates the joint, any tenseness present in the muscles will be lessened and its ability to work correctly and to its maximum extent will also be improved. It is this manipulation that can cause a clicking noise to be heard. As well as manipulation, other methods such as massage can be used to good effect. Muscles can be freed from tension if the tissue is massaged and this will also stimulate the flow of blood. In some cases, the patient may experience a temporary deterioration once treatment has commenced, and this is more likely to occur if the ailment has existed for quite some time.

People who have to spend a lot of their life driving are susceptible to a number of problems related to the manner in which they are seated in the car. If their position is incorrect they can suffer from tension headaches, pain in the back and the shoulders and the neck can feel stiff. There are a number of ways in which these problems can be remedied, such as holding the wheel in the approved manner (at roughly 'ten to two' on the dial of a clock). The arms should not be held out straight and stiff but should feel relaxed and with the arms bent at the elbow. In order that the driver can maintain a position in which the back and neck feel comfortable, the seat should be moved so that it is tilting backwards a little, although it should not be so far away that the pedals are not easily reached. The legs should not be held straight out, and if the pedals are the correct distance away the knees should be bent a little and feel quite comfortable. It is also important to sit erect and not slump in the seat. The driver's rear should be positioned right at the back of the seat, and this should be checked each time before using the vehicle. It is also important that there is adequate vision from the mirror so its position should be altered if necessary. If the driver already has a back problem then it is a simple matter to provide support for the lower part of the back. If this is done it should prevent strain on the shoulders and backbone. Whilst driving, the person should make a conscious effort to ensure that the shoulders are not tensed but held in a relaxed way. Another point to remember is that the chin should not be stuck out but kept in, otherwise the neck muscles

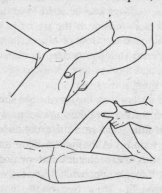

Osteopathic treatment of the knee

will become tensed and painful. Drivers can perform some beneficial exercises while they are waiting in a queue of traffic. To stretch the neck muscles, put the chin right down on to the chest and then relax. This stretching exercise should be done several times. There is another exercise that can also be done at the same time as driving and will have a positive effect on the flow of blood to the legs and also will improve how a person is seated. It is simply done by contraction and relaxation of the muscles in the stomach. Another exercise involves raising the shoulders upwards and then moving them backwards in a circular motion. The head should also be inclined forward a little. This should also be done several times to gain the maximum effect.

The figure on the previous page illustrates an example of diagnosis and treatment by manipulation, in which the osteopath examines a knee that has been injured. To determine the extent of the problem, the examination will be detailed and previous accidents or any other relevant details will be requested. If the practitioner concludes that osteopathy will benefit the patient, the joint will be manipulated so that it is able to function correctly and the manipulation will also have the effect of relaxing the muscles that have become tensed because of the injury.

Another form of therapy, which is known as cranial osteopathy, can be used for patients suffering from pain in the face or head. This is effected by the osteopath using slight pressure on these areas, including the upper part of the neck. If there is any tautness or tenseness present, the position is maintained while the problem improves. It is now common practice for doctors to recommend some patients to use osteopathy and some use the therapy themselves after receiving training. Although its benefits are generally accepted for problems of a mechanical nature, doctors believe it is vital that they first decide upon what is wrong before any use is made of osteopathy.

Polarity Therapy

Introduction

Origins

This is a therapy devised by Dr Randolph Stone (1890–1983) that amalgamates other healing therapies from both East and West. Dr Stone studied many of these therapies, including yoga (*see* page 195) and acupuncture (*see* page 7), and he was also trained to practise osteopathy (*see* page 82) and chiropractic (*see* page 28) among others. He began to search for a cure to a problem that he had experienced with some of his patients when, although their disorder had been cured by the use of manipulation, they subsequently became unwell. Through his studies of Eastern therapies he accepted the fundamental belief that a form of energy flows along certain channels in the body and that to keep good health the flow must be maintained. In India this energy is referred to as *prana* and in China it was called *chi* or *qi* The Western equivalent of this would probably be called a person's soul or spirit. It is believed that ailments occur when this flow of energy is blocked or is out of balance, and this could happen for different reasons, such as tension or stress, disturbances in the mind or unhealthy eating patterns. This energy is purported to be the controlling factor in a person's whole life and therefore affects the mind and body at all levels. It is believed that once the flow of energy has been restored to normal, the ailment will disappear and not recur.

The underlying belief

Dr Stone's polarity therapy states that there are three types of relationships, known as *neutral*, *positive* and *negative*, to be maintained between various areas in the body and five centres of energy. These centres originate from a very old belief held in India, and each centre is held to have an effect on its related part of the body. The centres are known as *ether* (controlling the ears and throat), *earth* (controlling the rectum and bladder), *fire* (controlling the stomach and bowels), *water* (controlling the pelvis and glands) and *air* (controlling the circulation and breathing). The therapy's aim is to maintain a balance and harmony between all these various points, and Dr Stone slowly developed four procedures to do this. They are the use of *diet*, *stretching exercises*, *touch and manipulation* and *mental attitude*, that is, contemplation allied with a positive view of life.

The treatment

Diet

To cleanse the body from a build-up of toxins caused by unhealthy eating and environmental pollution, the person will eat only fresh vegetables, fruit juices and fresh fruit. The length of time for this diet will vary according to the degree of cleansing required, but it is unlikely to be longer than a fortnight. Also available is a special drink that consists of lemon juice, olive oil, garlic and ginger. After the cleansing is complete, there is another diet to be followed that is said to promote and increase health, and finally one to ensure that the body maintains its level of good health.

Stretching exercises

Various positions may be adopted for the stretching exercises, such as on the floor with the legs crossed (A) or squatting or

A—sitting with the legs crossed

B—squatting

C—a change in the squatting position

sitting with the hands held at the back of the head. It is believed that these exercises free the channels that carry the body's energy and strengthen the sinews, muscles, ligaments and spine. As a way of releasing any stress or tension, the person would be requested to shout out loud at the same time as exercising. For the first exercise, the person can sit on the floor cross-legged with the right hand taking hold of the left ankle and with the left hand holding the right ankle. The eyes should then be shut and the mind relaxed and quiet.

For the squatting exercise, once in this position, clasp the hands out in front for balance and then move backwards and forwards and also in a circular motion. For people unable to balance in this position, a small book or similar item put under the heels should help (B).

For a slight change on the basic squatting position, bend the head forward and place the hands at the back of the neck so that the head and arms are between the knees. Relax the arms a little so that they drop forward slightly and thus the backbone is stretched (C).

Another variation is to hold the hands behind the neck whilst squatting and push the elbows and shoulder blades backwards and inwards. Any tension or stress can be relieved by shouting at the same time as breathing deeply.

Another exercise in which stress can be eased by shouting is known as the *wood chopper*. This is a fairly simple one to perform, and it entails standing with the feet apart and the knees bent. The hands should be clasped above the head as if about to chop some wood and the arms brought down together in a swinging action ending with the arms as far between the legs as possible. As the hands are being swung downwards, the person should shout, so that any tension is relieved. This action can be repeated quite frequently as long as there is no discomfort.

Touch and manipulation

Touch and manipulation are used by the therapist to detect any stoppages in the flow of energy along the channels, which are believed to be the reason for disorders. It is said that by the use of pressure, of which there are three sorts, the therapist is able to restore the flow of energy. *Neutral pressure* is gentle and calming and only the tips of the fingers are used. *Positive pressure* is the use of manipulation over the whole of the body with the exception of the head. *Negative pressure* is the use of a firmer and deeper manipulation and touch.

Mental attitude

Mental attitude is the fourth procedure, and basically this encourages people to have a more positive view on all aspects of their lives. This is achieved by talking or counselling sessions, and it is believed that a negative view of things can make a person more susceptible to having an ailment. A positive attitude is regarded as being essential for harmony in the body and mind.

Polarity therapy is claimed to be of some benefit to all people who are ill, although it does not concentrate on a particular set of symptoms but is more concerned with the overall aspect of the patient's health and the achievement of internal harmony and balance. For the therapy to work successfully, each patient has to believe in it completely and be prepared to carry out the practitioner's instructions with regard to diet, exercises, and so on. It is, of course, always advisable to make sure that any therapist is fully qualified before beginning treatment. At the first consultation, the patient will be required to give a complete case history to the therapist, who will then assess the flow of energy through the body and also check on its physical make-up. Reflexes such as the knee-jerk reflex are tested, and any imbalances or blockages in the energy channels are detected by the reflex and pressure point testing. If there is a stoppage or imbalance of the flow, this will be manifested by some physical symptoms. One way in which it is believed a patient can help to speed the restoration of health is by remembering and concentrating on any thoughts, feelings or pictures in the 'mind's eye' that happen while a particular area is being treated. The patient should also have knowledge of the body's ability to heal itself. If a patient is receiving treatment on a painful knee joint, for example, he or she should focus attention on that part of the body whilst being receptive to any feelings that occur. It is believed that if the patient is aware of the overall condition, as a complete person and not just the physical aspect, this will encourage restoration of health. It is possible that a patient will need to keep details of all food consumed to enable the practitioner to detect any harmful effects, and a 'fruit and vegetable' diet may be advised (as described previously). It may be that the patient has some habit, view or manner of life that is not considered conducive to good health. If this is the case, the patient would be able to take advantage of a counselling service in order to help make a change. Other alternative therapies such as the use of herbal medicine may be used to effect a cure.

Polarity therapy has much in common with other Eastern remedies that have the common themes of contemplation, exercise, touch or pressure and diet, and that can give much improvement. However, it is recommended that an accurate medical analysis of any condition is found in the first instance.

Reflexology

Introduction

Origins

Reflexology is a technique of diagnosis and treatment in which certain areas of the body, particularly the feet, are massaged to alleviate pain or other symptoms in the organs of the body. It is thought to have originated about 5,000 years ago in China and was also used by the ancient Egyptians. It was introduced to Western society by Dr William Fitzgerald, who was an ear, nose and throat consultant in America. He applied ten zones (or energy channels) to the surface of the body, hence the term 'zone therapy', and these zones, or channels, were considered to be paths along which flowed a person's vital energy, or 'energy force'. The zones ended at the hands and feet. Thus, when pain was experienced in one part of the body, it could be relieved by applying pressure elsewhere in the body, within the same zone.

Subsequent practitioners of reflexology have concentrated primarily on the feet, although the working of reflexes throughout the body can be employed to beneficial effect.

Massage and energy flow

Reflexology does not use any sort of medication—merely a specific type of massage at the correct locations on the body. The body's energy flow is thought to follow certain routes, connecting every organ and gland with an ending or pressure point on the feet, hands or another part of the body. When the available routes are blocked, and a tenderness on the body points to such a closure, then it indicates some ailment or condition in the body that may be somewhere other than the tender area. The massaging of particular reflex points enables these channels to be cleared, restoring the energy flow and at the same time healing any damage.

The uses of reflexology are numerous, and it is especially effective for the relief of pain (back pain, headaches and toothache), treatment of digestive disorders, stress and tension, colds and influenza, asthma, arthritis, and more. It is also possible to predict a potential illness and either give preventative therapy or suggest that specialist advice be sought. The massaging action of reflexology creates a soothing effect that enhances blood flow to the overall benefit of the whole body. Reflexology, however, clearly cannot be used to treat conditions that require surgery.

Reflex massage initiates a soothing effect to bring muscular and nervous relief. The pressure of a finger applied to a particular point (or nerve ending) may create a sensation elsewhere in the body, indicating the connection or flow between the two points. This is the basis of reflexology, and although pain may not be alleviated immediately, continued massage over periods of up to one hour will usually have a beneficial effect.

There are certain conditions for which reflexology is inappropriate, including diabetes, some heart disorders, osteoporosis, disorders of the thyroid gland and phlebitis (inflammation of the veins). It may also not be suitable for pregnant women or anyone suffering from arthritis of the feet.

The best way to undergo reflexology is in the hands of a therapist, who will usually massage all reflex areas, concentrating on any tender areas that will correspond to a part of the body that is ailing. Reflexology can, however, be undertaken at home on minor conditions such as back pain, headache, etc, but care should be taken not to over-massage any one reflex point as it may result in an unpleasant feeling. Although there have not been any clinical trials to ascertain the efficacy of reflexology, it is generally thought that it does little harm and, indeed, much benefit may result.

Some practitioners believe that stimulation of the reflex points leads to the release of endorphins (in a manner similar to acupuncture). Endorphins are compounds that occur in the brain and have pain-relieving qualities similar to those of morphine. They are derived from a substance in the pituitary gland and are involved in endocrine control (glands producing hormones, for example, the pancreas, thyroid, ovary and testis).

The reflexes

Reflexes on the hands and feet

Reflexes on the feet—the soles of the feet contain a large number of zones, or reflexes, that connect with organs, glands or nerves in the body, as shown in the diagrams on pages 97–98. In addition, there are a small number of reflexes on the top and insides of the feet, as shown in the diagrams on page 99.

The palms of the hands similarly contain a large number of reflex areas, reflecting the arrangement seen on the soles of the feet, as shown in the diagrams on pages 100–101. The backs of the hands again mirror, to some extent, the tops of the feet, containing a smaller number of reflex areas (*see* the diagrams on page 102).

Use of the hands in reflexology

The hands are considered to have an electrical property, so that the right-hand palm is positive and the left-hand palm is nega-

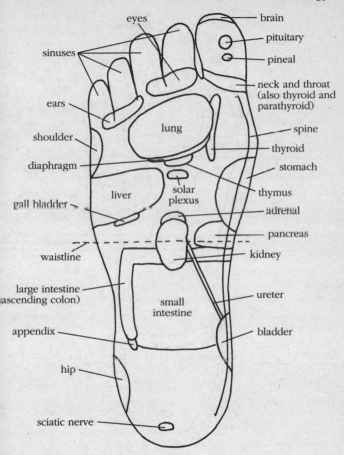

Major reflex points on the sole of the right foot

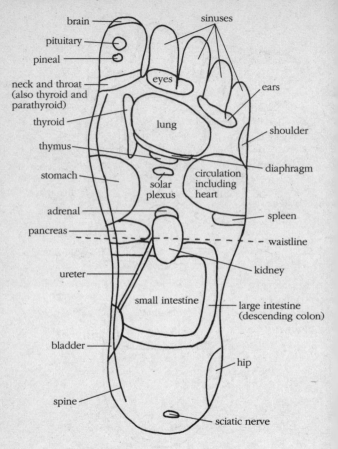

Major reflex points on the sole of the left foot

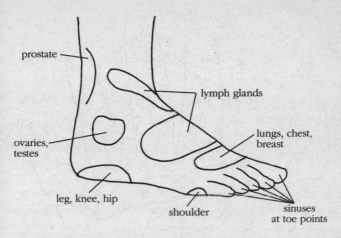

Reflex areas on the outside of the foot

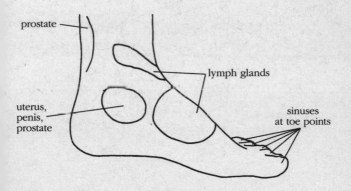

Reflex areas on the inside of the foot

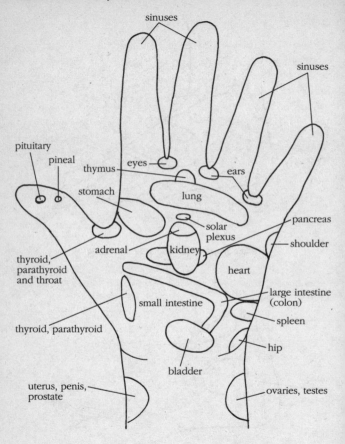

Major reflex points on the palm of the left hand

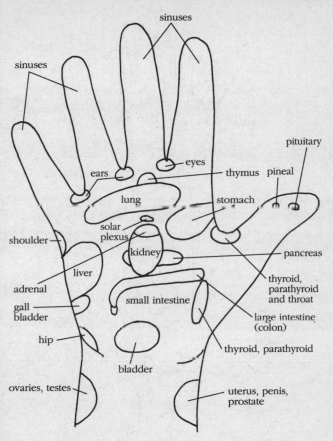

Major reflex points on the palm of the right hand

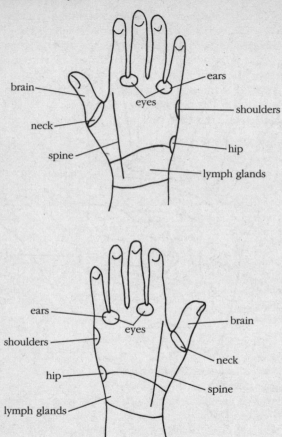

Reflexes on the backs of the hands

tive. In addition, the right hand has a reinforcing, stimulating effect while the left has a calming, sedative effect. The back of each hand is opposite to the palm, thus the right is negative and the left is positive. This is important when using reflexology because if the object is to revitalize the body and restore the energy flow that has been limited by a blockage then the right hand is likely to be more effective. The left hand, with its calming effect, is best used to stop pain.

Reflexes on the body

Reflexes on the body necessarily differ from those on the feet and hands in that there is less alignment with the ten zones (the diagrams on pages 104–105 show some of the reflexes on the body). Also, there are a number of reflex points on the body that correspond to several organs or glands. These reflex points are sometimes harder to find accurately and may be more difficult to massage.

The middle finger is thought to have the greatest effect, so this should be used to work the reflex point. Light pressure should be applied to each point, and if pain is felt it means there is a blockage or congestion somewhere. A painful point should be pressed until the discomfort subsides or for a few seconds at a time, a shorter rest being taken in between the applications of pressure.

The abdominal reflex

A general test can be applied by gently pressing into the navel, either with the middle finger or with one or both hands, with the individual lying in a supine position. The presence of a pulse or beat is taken to mean there is a problem in this area. To combat this, the same technique is used, holding for a few seconds (six or seven), releasing slightly, and keeping the fingers in the same area, gently massaging with a circular action. If it is nec-

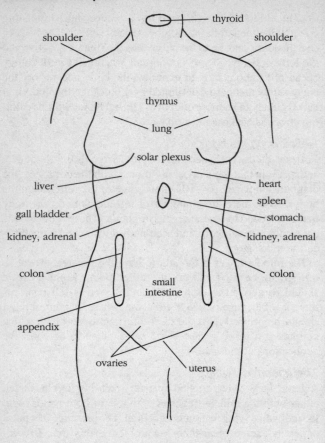

Major reflex areas on the body (female)

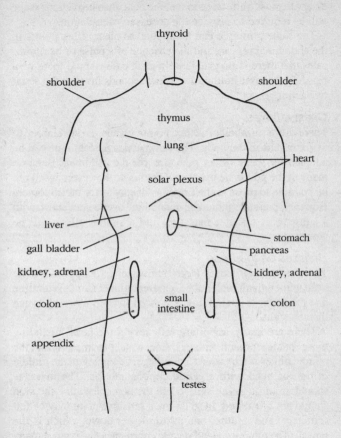

Major reflex areas on the body (male)

essary to press quite deep to feel the beat, then heavier massage will be required to provide the necessary stimulation.

The same principle can be applied to other reflex points in the abdominal region, and the absence of a pulse or beat indicates that there is no problem. In each case, should there be a painful response, holding for a few seconds invokes the sedative action.

Chest reflexes
There are a number of reflex points on the chest relating to major organs in the body. The same massage technique can be adopted for these reflex points as for the abdomen. Because many of the points lie over bone or muscle, however, it will not be possible to press in the finger as deeply as for the abdomen. However, pressure should be maintained over tender areas, with a subsequent circular massage, and a similar effect will be achieved.

Reflexes on the head
There are a surprisingly large number of reflex points on the head, although all may not be apparent immediately. With time and experience, such points are often located more by touch than by sight.

There are many important reflexes on the head, including those for the stomach, kidneys, spleen and pancreas. Again, the middle finger can be used for massage, beginning in the middle of the forehead with a gentle circular motion. The massage should go through the skin to rub the bone beneath—the skin should not be rubbed. In so doing, a sensitive point may be felt (pituitary) and another one a little lower down, which is the pineal. (The pituitary gland secretes hormones that control many body functions and the pineal body is thought to regulate the natural variations in the body's activities over a 24-hour pe-

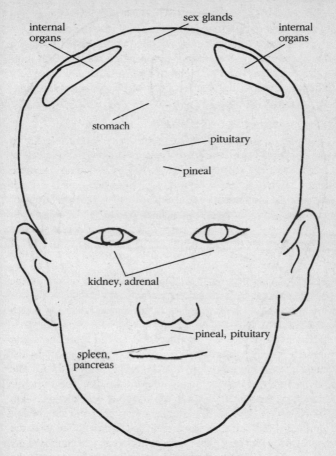

Some of the major reflex points on the head

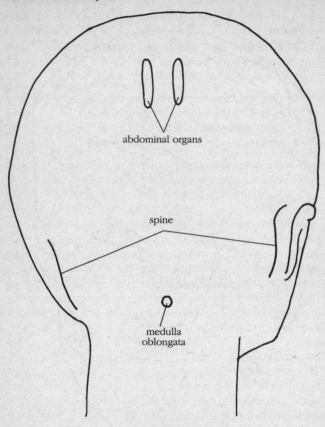

abdominal organs

spine

medulla
oblongata

*The back of the head to show the
medulla oblongata reflex*

riod.) This massaging action can be continued to check other parts of the body.

The back of the head also shows a large number of reflexes. However, there are a number of ways of stimulating the body as a whole through the head. These include:

(1) tapping the head gently with the fists, all over and very quickly for a period of about thirty seconds
(2) pulling handfuls of hair
(3) tapping the head gently with a wire brush

Each has a specific result; for example, stimulating the hair but also enlivening organs and glands over the whole body.

One particularly important reflex point is the medulla oblongata. The medulla oblongata is the lowest part of the brain stem, which joins to the upper part of the spinal cord. It contains important centres for the control of respiration, swallowing, salivation and the circulation. This reflex point is located at the nape of the neck, towards the base of the skull. Massage of this point opens all channels within the body and generates a vitality, relieving nervous tension and producing almost instant energy. The point should be pressed and massaged to produce the desired effects.

Ear reflexes

The ear has long been used in acupuncture because, in addition to its ease of use, it contains scores of acupoints, which correspond to the reflex points in reflexology. Some of these points are shown in the diagram on page 110.

The ear is perhaps the most difficult area of the body to work with because there are so many reflexes in such a small space. It becomes essentially a question of touch, pressing and exploring, and any sore point located can be massaged and worked

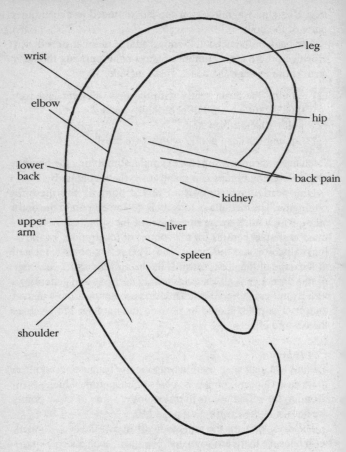

Some of the major reflex points on the ear

out. By using a gentle squeeze-and-roll method on the tops of the ears and the ear lobes a number of areas can be stimulated. It has been reported that reflexology can help ear problems such as ringing in the ears, and the condition tinnitus may be alleviated to some extent.

Techniques and practice

Some indication of the massaging, manipulative procedures of reflexology have already been mentioned, but a number of general points of guidance can also be made.

The whole process of reflexology is one of calm, gentle movements in a relaxed state. The foot is probably used most in reflexology, in which case shoes and socks and stockings, etc, should be removed. A comfortable position should be adopted on the floor or bed, in a warm, quiet room with the back supported by pillows.

To begin, the whole foot is massaged, indeed both feet should ideally be worked on. However, if working on your own feet it is thought that the right foot should be massaged first (contrary to previous practice). It is considered that the right foot is linked with the past, hence these emotions must be released before the present and future aspects are dealt with in the left foot.

Techniques of massage vary, but a simple method with which to start involves placing the thumb in the middle of the sole of the foot. The thumb then presses with a circular and rocking motion for a few seconds before moving to another reflex. Reference can be made to the diagrams on pages 97-98 to determine which reflex is being massaged. In all cases, the massage should work beneath the skin, not on the skin. Another method involves starting the massage with the big toe and then moving on to each toe in turn. In using the thumbs to effect the massage, some refinements of motion can be introduced to give slightly different movements:

(1) The thumb can be rocked between the tip and the ball, moving forwards over the relevant area. This, along with the circular massage already mentioned, relieves aches and pains.
(2) Both thumbs can be used alternately to stroke the skin firmly. This creates a calming effect.
(3) The area can be stroked with the thumbs, one moving over the other in a rotational sense. This action is intended to soothe and allow for personal development.

In addition to the procedures already mentioned, reflexology can be used to alleviate many symptoms and help numerous conditions. The following sections provide examples of these uses. Reflexology can be approached intuitively, so that the pressure of touch and the time factor can vary depending upon response and need.

The use of reflexology

The digestive system

The stomach is an organ that has thick muscular walls and in which food is reduced to an acidic semi-liquid by the action of gastric juices. There are many factors that can cause an upset stomach. To assess the general condition, the stomach body reflex (above the navel) can be pressed. Around it are several related reflexes, such as those for the liver, gall bladder, intestines and colon. The reflex should be pressed for a few seconds and then released three times to activate the reflex.

On the hands, the web of soft tissue between the thumb and forefinger of the left hand should be worked with the thumb of the right hand for a few minutes. The hands can be reversed but the stronger effect will be gained this way because the stomach lies mostly on the left side.

On the feet, the reflexes for the stomach are found primarily on the instep of the left foot, although they are also present on the right foot. These should be massaged, but there are further factors, in addition to the use of reflexology, that will aid digestion. These include eating a sensible diet with a minimum of artificial substances and not overeating. The use of certain essential oils (aromatherapy - *see* page 211) can also be of benefit. In this case peppermint oil can often be particularly effective.

The colon is the main part of the large intestine in which water and salts are removed from the food that enters from the small intestine. After extraction of the water, the waste remains are passed on to the rectum as faeces. If this system becomes unbalanced in any way then the water may not be absorbed or the food waste passes through the colon so quickly that water cannot be absorbed. In such cases, the result is diarrhoea, which can be painful and inconvenient.

Both body and foot reflexes should be massaged for the stomach, intestines, colon and also the liver and kidneys. The thyroid reflex should also be worked to help regulation of the body functions. A useful body reflex is to press and rotate your finger about 5cm (2 in) above the navel for a couple of minutes. This can be repeated numerous times, each time moving the fingers a little clockwise around the navel until a complete circuit has been made.

It is important that the condition be stabilized as soon as possible as continued loss also leads to loss of vital salts and a general nutritional deficiency.

At the outset it is possible to work the colon reflexes on the hand to identify any tender areas. The right thumb should be pressed into the edge of the pad (around the base and side of the thumb) of the left palm and worked around to seek out any tender spots. Any tender reflex should be massaged and pressed for a few seconds. In each case, the tenderness should be worked out. Since there are many reflex points crowded onto the navel, it may not solely be the colon reflex that requires some attention. It is always useful to work the reflex on both sides of the body to ensure a balance is achieved.

A similar approach can be adopted for reflexes on the feet, starting at the centre, or waistline. By applying a rolling pressure, the foot is massaged along to the inner edge and then down the line of the spine and any tender points are worked through pressure and massage. It may be necessary to start with a very light pressure if the area is very tender, and then as the soreness lessens, the pressure can be increased.

Again, diet can be an important factor in maintaining the health of the body and the workings of the colon. Fibre is particularly important in ensuring a healthy digestive system and avoiding ailments such as diverticulitis.

Reflexology can be used for other conditions associated with the digestive system, notably ulcers. A peptic ulcer (in the stomach, duodenum or even the oesophagus) is caused by a break in the mucosal lining. This may result from the action of acid, bile or enzymes because of unusually high concentrations or a deficiency in the systems that normally protect the mucosa. The result can be a burning sensation, belching and nausea.

To help alleviate the problem, which may often be stress-related, the reflexes in the feet should be massaged, as these are often the most relaxing. Obviously, the important reflexes are those for the stomach and duodenum, but it is also worthwhile to work on those for the liver and the endocrine glands (notably the pituitary). If the ulcer is a long-standing problem or if stomach complaints have been experienced for some time, then further medical help is probably needed.

The heart and circulatory system

The heart is obviously a vital organ. This muscular pump is situated between the lungs and slightly left of the midline. It projects forward and lies beneath the fifth rib. Blood returns from the body via the veins and enters the right atrium (the upper chamber), which contracts, forcing the blood into the right ventricle. From there it goes to the lungs where it gains oxygen and releases carbon dioxide before passing to the left atrium and left ventricle. Oxygenated blood then travels throughout the body via the arteries.

By using body reflexes, the heart can be maintained, and conditions can be dealt with by massaging the appropriate reflex points. A useful massage exercise is to work the muscles, rather than the reflex points, of the left arm in a side-to-side movement. This can be followed by the neck muscles and the chest muscles; in each case any tightness or tension should be massaged out. An additional preventative is a good diet, which should be low in fat and food that is high in cholesterol but should contain adequate amounts of vitamins, notably the B group, C and E. Exercise is, of course, very important to maintain a good heart and circulation.

There is also a simple test that many reflexologists feel is useful in the diagnosis of possible heart problems. It may also be worth doing if strenuous activity is contemplated in the near future. Pressure is applied to the pad of the left thumb, at the top. The pressure should be quite hard. It is suggested that when this part of the pad hurts, it indicates a constriction in blood vessels, limiting supply. If the bottom of the pad hurts, this is indicative of congested arteries. If the area is too tender to touch (and there is no physical damage to the hand) then there is a possibility of a heart attack. This test thus provides warning and enables a medical doctor to be consulted. Should painful areas occur on both hands, this does *not* indicate a heart problem.

Many blood and circulatory disorders will benefit from the same sort of massage. In these cases the foot reflexes for the endocrine glands (hypothalamus, pituitary, pineal, thyroid and parathyroid, thymus, adrenals, pancreas, ovary or testis) should be worked well, as should those for the circulatory system and heart, lungs and lymphatic system.

Conditions that may benefit from such treatment include:

Angina
Any suffocating, choking pain but the word is usually used to refer to angina pectoris, which is felt in the chest and occurs when blood supply to the heart muscle is inadequate. It is brought on by exercise and relieved by rest. The coronary arteries may be damaged by atheroma (scarring and buildup of fatty deposits). Of particular importance are the heart and circulatory reflexes (veins and arteries) and those of the lymphatic system.

Arteriosclerosis
A general term including atheroma and atherosclerosis (where arteries degenerate and fat deposits reduce blood flow), which results generally in high blood pressure and can lead to angina. Additional reflexes that should be worked include the liver.

Hypertension (high blood pressure)
This may be one of several types, the commonest being *essential* (the result of kidney or endocrine disease or an unknown cause)

and *malignant* (a serious condition that tends to occur in the younger age groups). In addition to the reflexes for the blood and circulation, those for the shoulders, neck and eyes should be worked in combination with reflexes for the digestive system and liver.

Palpitations

An irregular heartbeat, often associated with heightened emotions, but also caused by heart disease and may be felt during pregnancy. The lung and heart reflexes are particularly important, in addition to those of the circulation.

Some heart conditions are very serious and require immediate hospitalization, e.g. cardiac arrest (when the heart stops) and coronary thrombosis. (The latter is a coronary artery blockage causing severe chest pain, vomiting, nausea and breathing difficulties. The affected heart muscle dies, a condition known as myocardial infarction.) However, massage of appropriate reflexes may help, particularly in less serious cases. These should include those for the heart and circulation (veins and arteries), lungs, endocrine system and the brain. Each will have some beneficial effect in relieving stress and congestion.

Varicose veins

Veins that have become stretched, twisted and distended, often occuring in the superficial veins in the legs. The possible causes are numerous and include pregnancy, defective valves, obesity and thrombophlebitis (the inflammation of the wall of a vein with secondary thrombosis). Phlebitis is inflammation of a vein and occurs primarily as a complication of varicose veins. Both these conditions can be treated by massaging the circulatory reflexes and also the leg and liver reflexes. In both cases, resting with the legs in an elevated position is beneficial.

The respiratory system

Asthma is one of the major problems of the respiratory system and its incidence seems to be escalating. The condition is caused by a narrowing of the airways in the lungs. It usually begins in early childhood and may be brought on by exposure to allergens (substances, usually proteins, that cause allergic reactions) exercise or stress.

There are certain body reflexes that can help in this instance. One reflex point is in the lower neck at the base of the V-shape created by the collar bones. Relief may be achieved by pressing the finger into this point with a downward motion for a few seconds. There are additional reflex points on the back, at either side of the spine in the general region of the shoulder blades. These can be worked by someone else with thumb or finger, which should be pressed for a few seconds. Other reflexes that can be worked on the foot include those for the brain, endocrine glands such as the pineal, pituitary, thymus and thyroid, the lungs and also the circulatory system. Particular attention should be paid to those for the lungs, which include the bronchi and bronchioles, the branching passageways of the lungs where gaseous exchange (oxygen in, carbon dioxide out) takes place. At the point where the instep meets the hard balls of the feet and along the base of the lung reflex area is the massage point for the diaphragm. Working the whole of this area will help alleviate symptoms of asthma. During an attack of asthma, both thumbs can be placed on the solar plexus reflexes immediately to initiate the soothing process.

The adrenal glands are found one to each kidney, situated on the upper surface of that organ. These are important endocrine glands because they produce hormones such as adrenaline and cortisone. Adrenaline is very important in controlling the rate of respiration and it is used medically in the treatment of bron-

chial asthma because it relaxes the airways. It is clear, therefore, that the adrenal reflex is an important one and it is located
in the middle of each sole and palm.

Many other respiratory disorders can be helped by using
massage of the same reflexes: those of the brain, endocrine
glands, lungs and diaphragm, neck and shoulders, augmented
by those of the heart and circulatory system. Conditions responding to this regime include bronchitis, croup, lung disorders and emphysema (distension and thinning, particularly of
lung tissue, leading to air-filled spaces that do not contribute to
the respiratory process).

Infections of the respiratory tract leading to coughs and colds
can also be helped primarily by working the reflexes mentioned
above. For colds, the facial reflexes should be massaged, especially that for the nose. However, it is good practice to include
the pituitary reflex and to work the index and middle fingers
towards the tip to help alleviate the condition.

With such respiratory problems, there are complementary
therapies that can help such as homeopathy (*see* page 234),
aromatherapy (*see* page 211) and Bach flower remedies (*see*
page 162). There are also many simple actions that can be taken;
for example, a sore throat may be helped by gargling regularly
with a dessertspoon of cider apple vinegar in a glass of water,
with just a little being swallowed each time. Honey is also a good
substance to take, as are onion and garlic.

The endocrine glands

The role of the glands
Endocrine glands are glands that release hormones directly into
the bloodstream or lymphatic system. Some organs, such as the

pancreas, also release secretions via ducts. The major endocrine glands are, in addition to the pancreas, the pituitary, pineal, thyroid, parathyroid, thymus, adrenal and gonads (ovaries and testes).

The endocrine glands are of vital importance in regulating body functions, as summarized below:

pituitary	controls growth, gonads, kidneys; known as the master gland
pineal	controls the natural daily rhythms of the body
thyroid	regulates metabolism and growth
parathyroid	controls calcium and phosphorus metabolism
thymus	vital in the immune system, particularly pre-puberty
adrenal	control of heartbeat, respiration and metabolism
gonads	control of reproductive activity
pancreas	control of blood sugar levels

The fact that the endocrine glands are responsible for the very core of body functions means that any imbalance should be corrected immediately to restore normality. There are some general points relating to massage of these reflex areas. It is good practice to massage the brain reflex first and then that of the pituitary. This is because the hypothalamus, situated in the forebrain, controls secretions from the pituitary gland. The reflexes should be gently massaged with thumb or finger for a few seconds and then gentle pressure exerted and held for a few seconds before releasing slowly.

The pituitary

An imbalance of pituitary gland secretions, often caused by a benign tumour, can lead to acromegaly (excessive growth of skeletal and soft tissue). Gigantism can result if it occurs during adolescence. There may also be consequent deficiencies in adrenal, gonad and thyroid activity. The brain and endocrine reflexes should be worked in order, supplemented by those for the circulation, liver and digestion. In addition to reflex points on the hands and feet, there is also one on the forehead. If any of these reflex areas is found to be tender, it should be massaged often to maintain the balance necessary for healthy growth.

The pineal

The pineal body, or gland, is situated on the upper part of the mid-brain, although its function is not fully understood. It would seem, however, to be involved in the daily rhythms of the body and may also play a part in controlling sexual activity. The pineal reflex points are found close to those of the pituitary on the big toes, the thumbs and on the forehead and upper lip.

The thyroid

The thyroid is located at the base of the neck and produces two important hormones, thyroxine and triiodothyronine. Under- or overactivity of the thyroid leads to specific conditions.

If the thyroid is overactive and secretes too much thyroxine (hyperthyroidism), the condition called thyrotoxicosis develops. It is also known as Grave's disease and is typified by an enlarged gland, protruding eyes and symptoms of excess metabolism such as tremor, hyperactivity, rapid heart rate, breathlessness, etc. The important reflexes on which to concentrate are those for the brain and solar plexus, the endocrine system and also the circulatory and digestive systems. The reflexes are found on the soles and palms; using the thumbs or fingers, the areas should be massaged but in stages if the area is very tender.

Underactivity of the thyroid, or hypothyroidism, can cause myxoedema, producing dry, coarse skin, mental impairment, muscle pain and other symptoms. In children a similar lack causes cretinism, resulting in dwarfism and mental retardation. The reflexes to be worked are essentially those mentioned for hyperthyroidism, and in addition (for both conditions) the liver reflexes on the right sole and palm should benefit from attention.

There are additional thyroid reflexes elsewhere on the body, notably on the neck roughly midway between jaw and collarbone and on either side. These points should be massaged gently with the thumb and fingers on opposite sides of the throat. Using a gentle gyratory motion, the massage can be taken down to the collarbone. The fingers and thumb of the other hand are then used (on opposite sides of the throat) and the procedure repeated.

Goitre is another condition associated with the thyroid. It is a swelling of the neck caused by enlargement of the gland, typically the result of overactivity of the gland to compensate for an iodine deficiency. The important reflexes to concentrate upon are those for the brain, solar plexus, endocrine system and circulatory system but working all the body reflexes will help.

The parathyroid

There are four small parathyroid glands located behind or within the thyroid. They control the use of calcium and phosphorus (as phosphate) in the body's metabolism. An imbalance of these vital elements can lead to tetany (muscular spasms) or, at the other extreme, calcium may be transferred from the bones to the blood, creating a tendency to bone fractures.

The reflexes for these glands are found in the same location as those for the thyroid but it will probably be necessary to massage more strongly to achieve an effect. It is a good idea to work on these areas each time reflexology is undertaken as they are vital in maintaining the metabolic equilibrium of the body.

The thymus

The thymus is located in the neck (over the breastbone) and is a vital contributor to the immune system. It is larger in children and is important in the development of the immune response. After puberty it shrinks although it seems to become more active later in life. Bone marrow cells mature within the thymus, and one group, T-lymphocytes, are dependent upon the presence of the thymus. These are important cells as they produce antibodies.

The commonest disorder associated with the thymus is myasthenia gravis, which lowers the level of acetylcholine (a neurotransmitter), resulting in a weakening of skeletal muscles and those used for breathing, swallowing, etc. The thymus reflexes are found on the soles of the feet and palms of the hand, next to the lung reflexes. The thymus can also be stimulated by tapping with the finger over its reflex area in the middle of the upper chest.

The adrenals

The two adrenals (also known as suprarenals) are situated one above each kidney and consist of an inner medulla and an outer cortex. The medulla produces adrenaline, which increases the rate and depth of respiration, raises the heartbeat and improves muscle performance, with a parallel increase in output of sugar from the liver into the blood.

The cortex of the adrenal glands releases hormones, including aldosterone, which controls the balance of electrolytes in the body, and cortisone, which, among other functions, is vital in the response to stress, inflammation and fat deposition in the body.

On both the palms and soles, the adrenal reflexes are located above those for the kidneys, and if this area is at all tender, it should be massaged for a few seconds. Because the kidney and adrenal reflexes are close together, the massage should be limited to avoid over-stimulation of the kidney reflexes. Disorders of the adrenal glands should be treated by working the endocrine reflexes, starting with the pituitary and including the adrenal reflexes themselves, followed by the reflexes for the circulatory, liver and urinary systems.

Specific disorders include Cushing's syndrome, caused by an overproduction of cortisone, which results in obesity, reddening of the face and neck, growth of body and facial hair, high blood pressure, osteoporosis and possibly mental disturbances, and Addison's disease, which results from damage to the cortex and therefore a deficiency in hormone secretion. The latter was commonly caused by tuberculosis but now by disturbances in the immune system. The symptoms are weakness, wasting, low blood pressure and dark pigmentation of the skin. Both these conditions can be treated by hormone replacement therapy, but reflexology can assist through massage of the endocrine, digestive and liver reflexes.

The gonads

The gonads, or sex glands, comprise the ovaries in women and testes in men. The ovaries produce eggs and also secrete hormones, mainly oestrogen and progesterone. Similarly, the testes produce sperm and the hormone testosterone. Oestrogen controls the female secondary sexual characteristics such as enlargement of the breasts, growth of pubic hair and deposition of body fat. Progesterone is vital in pregnancy as it prepares the uterus for implantation of the egg cell.

The reflexes for these and related organs are found near the ankles on the inside of the feet, just below the angular bone (*see* figure depicting the reflex areas on the inside and outside of the feet on page 99). The same reflex areas are also located on the arms, near the wrist. The ovaries and testes are on the outer edge, while on the opposite, inner edge are the reflexes for the uterus, penis and prostate.

For any disorders that might involve the ovaries or testes, it is also useful to massage other reflexes such as those for the brain, other endocrine glands, the circulation and liver.

The pancreas

This is an important gland with both endocrine and exocrine functions. It is located behind the stomach, between the duodenum and spleen. The exocrine function involves secretion of pancreatic juice, via ducts, into the intestine. The endocrine function is vital in balancing blood sugar levels through the secretion of two hormones, insulin and glucagon. Insulin controls the uptake of glucose by body cells, and a lack of hormone results in the sugar derived from food being excreted in the urine, the condition known as diabetes mellitus. Glucagon works in the opposite sense to insulin and increases the supply of blood sugar through the breakdown of glycogen in the liver to produce glucose.

The primary reflexes for the pancreas are found on the soles and palms, near to the stomach. The thumb should be used, starting on the left foot, working across the reflex area and on to the right foot. If the area is tender, it should be worked until the tenderness goes. Because there are numerous reflexes in this area, there will be stimulation of other organs, to the general wellbeing of the body as a whole.

For other disorders of the pancreas, such as pancreatitis (inflammation of the pancreas), the reflexes associated with digestion should also be worked. Pancreatitis may result from gallstones or alcoholism and, if sufficiently severe, may cause diabetes.

The liver and spleen

The role of the liver

The liver is a very important organ and is critical in regulating metabolic processes. It is the largest gland in the body and is situated in the top right-hand part of the abdominal cavity. Among its functions, the liver converts excess glucose to glycogen, which is stored as a food reserve; excess amounts of amino acids are converted into urea for excretion; bile is produced for storage in the gall bladder and some poisons are broken down. The liver also recycles red blood cells to remove the iron when the cells reach the end of their life; it stores vitamins and produces blood-clotting substances. Because of its high chemical and biochemical activity, the liver generates a lot of heat and is the major contributor of heat to the body.

The liver reflex points

The reflex area for the liver is a large area, reflecting the size of the organ, on the right palm and right sole, on the outer edge. As a general procedure, the area should be massaged with the left thumb, searching for tender points. More massage may be required for the liver than for other reflexes.

Hepatitis is inflammation of the liver caused by viral infection or the presence of toxins. Alcohol abuse commonly causes hepatitis, and it may also result from drug overdose or drug side effects. Viral infections such as HIV and glandular fever can also cause hepatitis. There are several types of hepatitis, designated A to E, and all may persist in the blood for a long time.

To combat such disorders, after removing the source of any toxins, the reflex for the liver and digestion should be worked and the reflexes for the eyes. Dietary restraint is also important and should involve natural foods with little or no alcohol, caffeine or nicotine and a low intake of fats.

The gall bladder

Associated with the liver anatomically is the gall bladder. This is a small sac-like organ that stores and concentrates bile. When fats are digested, the gall bladder contracts, sending bile into the duodenum. Sometimes stones form here, and gallstones can often cause severe pain. The gall bladder reflex is found at the foot of the liver reflex on the right palm and foot. On the body there is another reflex just below the ribs on the right-hand side and below the liver reflex point. A steady pressure should be held around the point, beginning near the navel and working to the right side maintaining pressure for a few seconds on any tender point.

The role of the spleen

The spleen is situated on the left side of the body, behind and below the stomach. The spleen produces leucocytes (white blood cells), lymphocytes (white blood cells involved in the immune system), blood platelets (involved in blood coagulation) and plasma cells. It also acts as a store for red blood cells, which are made available in emergencies (when oxygen demand is greater).

The spleen reflex point

The reflex area for the spleen is found on the left palm or sole, below the reflex for the heart. If a tender point is found in this reflex, it may indicate anaemia and it would then be wise to obtain a blood test.

The kidneys and bladder

The role of the kidneys and bladder

The kidneys are important organs in the body's excretory system. They are responsible for processing the blood continuously to remove nitrogenous wastes (mainly urea) and they also adjust salt concentrations. By testing the reflexes with the thumb, tender areas can be located and worked upon. However, prolonged massage should be avoided—it is better to use shorter periods of 15–20 seconds initially as the system becomes accustomed to the treatment.

It is not surprising, considering the pivotal role of the kidneys in removing body wastes, that any interference with their normal function can lead to serious illnesses. General kidney disorders, kidney stones, nephritis and pyelitis are all best aided by massaging the kidney reflex but also the reflexes for the central nervous system, the endocrine glands (especially the pituitary and adrenal glands), liver, stomach and circulation. Kidney stones are formed by the deposition of solid substances that are naturally found in the urine but that precipitate out for one reason or another. They are commonly salts of calcium, and the alteration in pH of the urine is often a contributory factor. Nephritis is inflammation of the kidney and pyelitis is when part of the kidney, the pelvis, becomes inflamed. If the whole kidney becomes affected, it is then called pyelonephritis.

The kidney and bladder reflex points
Disorders associated with the bladder tend to be infections such as cystitis or other physical manifestation of a problem whether through stress or a medical condition. The latter category includes enuresis (bed-wetting) and incontinence. In these cases, the bladder reflex should obviously be worked upon and the reflexes for the brain, solar plexus and endocrine system.

The reflexes for the kidneys are found just off-centre on the palms of both hands and soles of both feet. They are close to those for the pancreas and stomach. The bladder reflex is towards the base of the palm, near the wrist, and on the feet it is found on the inside edge of both soles, towards the heel. There are also body reflexes for both organs.

The body reflexes for the kidney are at the side of the body, almost at the waistline, between the hip and rib cage. They also occur on the face, just beneath the eyes.

The alleviation of back pain and other skeletal disorders

The reflex points for the spine

Within the working population of most countries, back pain accounts for millions of days in lost production. This is not unexpected as the spine is the primary part of the skeleton, hence any problem with it will inevitably upset the body and its overall wellbeing.

The reflex for the spine is located on the soles of the feet, along the inner edge of both feet, running from the base of the big toe almost to the heel. By working this line with the fingers, any tender points can be found and worked upon. The top end of the line, near the toe, is equivalent to the spine at the level of the shoulders.

Treatment of back disorders through reflexology

With back disorders, such as lumbago, additional reflexes should be worked, including those for the brain and endocrine system. Because the body's musculature is a complementary and antagonistic system, with the skeleton creating all the movements of which the body is capable, the muscles are also important when dealing with back pain. It will help therefore to massage muscles, rubbing quite deeply with the fingers and moving across the muscles.

Back pain can result from a problem elsewhere in the body caused by bad posture, tight muscles or even flat feet. It is important to be aware of the possibilities and ensure that the treatment deals with the problem as a whole and not just in part. Exercise is clearly beneficial and walking can help loosen and strengthen muscles associated with the back. A brisk walk is fine, but jogging is not necessarily the best remedy as in some cases this can itself prove harmful.

Reflexologists often turn to the muscles in the legs to alleviate back pain, particularly in the area of the lower back. The muscles at the back of the thigh should be massaged with a pressing and pulling action, first with one hand and then the other. The whole of the thigh should be treated, from the top of the leg to the knee. Massage of both legs in this manner, concentrating on any 'tight' areas, will help improve the overall tone and assist in eliminating causes of back pain.

Study of the diagrams for the feet and hands reveals specific reflex areas for the shoulders, hip and neck. When working on skeletal disorders in general, it is wise to undertake a thorough massage of specific reflex areas, such as those for the neck and shoulders plus those for the brain, solar plexus, the endocrine system, remainder of the skeletal system, endocrine glands, etc. For particular conditions such as bursitis (inflammation of a joint, as in housemaid's knee), general joint pain, stiff neck and similar complaints, a common regime of reflexological massage applies. This should include working the skeletal reflexes along with those for the nervous and endocrine system, digestive and circulatory systems. It is usually the case that the specific complaint will benefit from massage of its reflex area and most of those that comprise a whole-body workout. It should always be remembered that there are occasions when surgery may prove essential, e.g. in the case of a hip replacement.

The knee joint can often be the source of pain and discomfort. It may help to apply gentle pressure on either side of the knee, just where the bone ends, using the thumb and middle finger. This should be held for a few seconds, pressing as much as possible (do not press hard if it is too painful) and then the same should be done below the knee.

Relief from arthritis with reflexology

Arthritis can be a crippling disease and many people suffer from it. It is an inflammation of joints or the spine, the symptoms of which are pain and swelling, restriction of movement, redness and warmth of the skin. Two forms of the condition are osteoarthritis and rheumatoid arthritis.

Treatment of osteoarthritis through reflexology

Osteoarthritis involves the cartilage in joints, which then affects the associated bone. What often happens is that the cartilage is lost, to be replaced by osteophytes at the edges of the bones. These are bony projections that occur with the loss of cartilage or with age. The projections affect the joint function, causing pain.

Treatment of rheumatoid arthritis through reflexology

Rheumatoid arthritis is the second commonest joint disease after osteoarthritis. It usually affects the feet, ankles, wrists and fingers in which there is a swelling of the joint and inflammation of the synovial membrane (the membraneous envelope around the joint). Then follows erosion and loss of cartilage and loss of bone. At its worst, the condition can be disabling.

Massage of the reflex areas for the affected areas should be worked but, as mentioned previously, it is important to massage the reflexes for the whole body to achieve a complete and balanced approach. The endocrine system is one important system in this respect.

131

In seeking ways to treat rheumatoid arthritis, the medical profession isolated the glucocorticosteroid hormone, cortisone, from the adrenal glands of cattle. It was found that the use of cortisone had dramatic effects on the symptoms of rheumatoid arthritis. However, the relief was only temporary, and an additional disadvantage was the occurrence of associated side effects, which could be severe, e.g. damage to muscle and bone, stomach ulcers, bleeding and imbalances in the hormonal and nervous systems. The medical use of this compound is therefore very restricted, but it is produced naturally by the adrenal cortex. Being a natural secretion, there are no detrimental side effects. There is a reflex point in the lower back, between the first and second lumbar vertebrae, which can be pressed. Finding this point will be hit and miss initially, but upon locating it —roughly 5 cm (2 in) up from the coccyx or tailbone—apply gentle pressure, gradually increasing, and hold it for a few seconds. This should be repeated several times. This is helpful for other conditions in addition to rheumatoid arthritis, such as asthma and bursitis.

As with back disorders, muscle condition is also felt to be important in the treatment of arthritis. The muscles in the area affected by arthritis should be massaged by pressing in with the fingers, either on or near to the area. The massage should be across the muscles, with a deep motion, although it may initially produce discomfort or soreness. Many practitioners regard this as an important supplementary technique in administering reflexology.

Stress and tension

The relaxing effects of reflexology
One of the additional beneficial effects of reflexology when

dealing with a particular reflex area or point is that the treatment is very relaxing. If most of the body reflexes are massaged, a feeling of wellbeing is generated and tension is released. Stress control and relief can be accomplished in a number of ways, some of which happen instinctively, such as deep breathing and, paradoxically, wringing the hands. The latter is an obvious way of working the reflex points, albeit that it is mostly done unconsciously. A related method of calming the nerves is to intertwine the fingers, as in clasping the hands, which enables all the reflexes between the fingers to be pressed. This should be done several times. Deep breathing is a common method of relaxation that ultimately can envelop the whole body, providing that the focus of attention is the attainment of the correct pattern of breathing. Mental attitude is also an important aspect of reflexology. It clearly makes sense while undergoing massage (with or without a practitioner or partner) to imagine, or listen to, pleasing sounds rather than worrying about the pressures of modern life. If there is no access to relaxing sounds (bird song, running water, etc) it is perfectly possible to imagine it and thereby to augment the physical relaxation with mental calm.

Reflex points for treating stress

The endocrine glands are considered important in combating stress because they are responsible for the hormonal balance of the body. All reflex areas for these glands, on both soles and palms, should be massaged and special attention given to the thyroid, which controls body temperature and can help restore calm. The adrenal reflex point, almost in the centre of the hand, is also important, and, because it is so near the solar plexus, receives equal attention. (The solar plexus is a network of nerves and ganglia in the sympathetic nervous system concerned with body functions not under conscious control. It is located behind the stomach.)

Quite often stress and tension can result in a sore neck or back. A number of reflex points can be worked to relieve these sorts of complaint. The medulla oblongata is important in this respect as it controls some major body functions such as the circulation. The point on the back of the head (*see* the diagram on page 108) should be held with the middle finger for a few seconds and then released, and repeated several times. The reflex points of the spine should also be worked, starting at the neck reflex, which is found below the base of the big toe or thumb. By moving down the side of the foot, the whole spine can be covered. To relieve a sore back completely and effectively, other reflexes to be attended to should include those for the shoulders, hips, and the sciatic nerve. The sciatic nerve is made up of a number of nerve roots from the lower part of the spinal cord, and pain with this origin may be felt in the back of the thigh, buttock and the foot. The reflex point may at first be painful to the touch, but through careful massage it can be worked to assist in promoting relief.

Control of the heart rate is a natural, complementary procedure in promoting stress relief. If a situation, wherever it may be, results in you feeling stressed, massaging the reflex areas for the heart will help, whether on foot or hand.

Sound, restful sleep is refreshing and also contributes to a reduction in stress. Reflexology can also help in this respect through the feeling of relaxation that it induces. The clasping of the hands, mentioned earlier, can be used to combat sleeplessness. The fingers can be clasped on the chest and then worked over each other so that the length of each finger is massaged. The fingers should remain intertwined and simply be released a little to allow each finger over the first knuckle when the fingers are squeezed together again. This, associated with deep breathing, will encourage relaxation.

Reflexology and the reproductive system

Reflex points for the reproductive system

The major reflexes of the reproductive system are those for the uterus, ovary and breast in the female, and the penis, testes and prostate in the male. The ovary reflexes are found on the outer side of the foot, just below the ankle (*see* diagrams on page 99). On the hand, these are found a little way beyond the wrist (*see* diagrams on page 102), on the outer edge. On both foot and hand, the breast reflex is found on the outer edge, a little below the base of the little toe or finger. The uterus reflex on the hand occupies a position opposite to the ovaries, i.e. just below the wrist but on the inner edge of the arm. On the foot, this reflex mirrors that for the ovary, but it is on the inside of the foot, below the ankle.

The male reflexes

The male reflexes occupy the same positions as those of the female, thus the penis reflex is in the same position as that for the uterus and the testes is the same as the ovaries. The prostate gland reflexes are situated with the penis reflex and also at the back of the leg/foot, above the heel (*see* the diagrams on page 99).

There are also reflex points on the head for the gonads (*see* sex glands on the diagram of the reflex points on the head on page 107). As well as working the various reflexes for the reproductive system, it is beneficial to pay attention to the endocrine gland reflexes as they have considerable control over the gonads (*see* endocrine glands, page 119). In particular, the pituitary, thyroid and adrenal glands and their hormonal secretions have a large influence on the reproductive system. All these points should be massaged to stimulate activity and ensure that hormone secretion is balanced and gonad activity is normal. The body reflexes can also be used to this end by pressing each point for a few seconds and repeating several times for all endocrine and sex glands.

If an endocrine gland is tender, it may indicate a problem with the sex glands. By working the various reflex points, it is possible to ensure a healthy reproductive system. There are a number of reflexes for the penis and testes that can help in this respect. The sex reflex below the navel should be pressed with fingers or thumb and massaged for a few seconds. Additional reflex points on the legs, about 15 cm (5 in) above the ankle on the inside of the leg, should also be massaged. Initially massage here should be for half a minute or so because any problems will make it tender. However, with further attention it will be possible to work out the soreness. A further point on the leg lies above the knee, in the soft area on the outer edge above the kneecap. All these reflexes, if worked in turn, will contribute to a healthy system and lead to fewer problems, such as impotence.

Impotence itself can, however, be treated. In addition to undertaking the massage of reflex points and areas mentioned above, there are further techniques that may help. There is a particularly sensitive and stimulating area between the anus and scrotum that should be pressed gently a number of times. It is also said that if gentle on-off pressure is applied to the scrotum, this will help.

Another problem faced by many men involves the prostate gland. This gland is situated below the bladder and opens into the urethra, which is the duct carrying urine out of the body and which also forms the ejaculatory duct. On ejaculation, the gland secretes an alkaline fluid into the sperm to help sperm motility. In older men particularly, the prostate gland may have become enlarged, causing problems with urination. Working the appropriate reflexes may help this situation, as may massaging the base of the penis. However, it is advisable to check with a doctor to ensure that there is no other condition present.

The female reflexes

There are a number of female conditions that may be helped by reflexology. In most cases, the reflexes to be worked are very similar and the following complaints are therefore grouped in this way:

(1) *amenorrhoea* lack of menstruation, other than during pregnancy or pre-puberty

(2) *endometriosis* the occurrence of endometrial cells, normally found in the womb, elsewhere in the body, e.g. Fallopian tubes or peritoneum, causing pain and bleeding

(3) *fibroid* a benign tumour of the uterus that may cause pain, bleeding and urine retention

(4) *leucorrhoea* discharge of white/yellow mucus from the vagina, which may be normal before and after menstruation, but at other times large amounts signify an infection

(5) *dysmenorrhoea* painful menstruation

(6) *menorrhagia* excessive blood flow during menstruation

For these and related conditions, the general procedure should be to spend time on the specific female reflex, which in these cases is the uterus reflex. In addition the endocrine gland reflexes should be massaged, and to provide a balanced treatment, the reflexes for the other reproductive organs (ovary, etc) should be worked. Further reflex areas to concentrate upon include those for the urinary and circulatory systems and the central nervous system (brain) with the solar plexus.

Premenstrual tension (or syndrome) is the condition typified by headache, nervousness, irritability, depression and tiredness (in addition to physical symptoms) several days before the start of menstruation. It is advisable, before menstruation starts, to have a thorough massage of the reflexes once or twice per week. Next, the reflexes for the uterus and ovaries should be worked. The uterus reflex is on the inside of the foot in the soft area beneath the ankle. The massage should work all around the ankle, beginning with a gentle pressure and then working back towards the heel. The other foot should then be dealt with in the same way.

To help overcome depression the endocrine glands are very important to regulate hormones, maintain body rhythms and balance the biochemical functions—all of which have some effect on emotions. Other reflexes to work, in addition to those for the endocrine glands, include those for the solar plexus, brain and liver. The liver reflex is very important in this respect, and although the area should not be overworked, it should not be forgotten.

The menopause is the time when a woman's ovaries no longer release an egg cell every month and child-bearing is no longer possible. This usually occurs between the ages of 45 and 55. It may be preceded by a gradual decline in the frequency of menstruation or there may be an abrupt cessation. There is an imbalance in the sex hormones, and this can cause a number of symptoms, including hot flushes, sweats, palpitations, depression and vaginal dryness. Over a longer period there may be a gradual loss of bone (osteoporosis) leading to a greater risk of bone fractures.

In this instance, the endocrine reflexes are once again very important. In conjunction with these, the reflexes for the spine and brain should be worked, the former to promote relaxation. As a general point, the reflexes for the spine can be massaged for any length of time whereas those for organs and glands should be worked periodically and for a few seconds each time.

To help combat hot flushes, the thyroid reflex should be worked since this is the endocrine gland responsible for the control of the metabolic rate. Regulation of breathing through deep breaths will also help.

The breasts are, of course, the mammary glands that produce milk at the appropriate time, but in today's society they have also become important from a cosmetic point of view. Disorders of the breasts can include lumps or cysts, pain or tenderness. Such conditions may be caused by an hormonal imbalance but in any event will benefit from a complete treatment of all the reflexes on feet, hands or head. The breast reflex is found on the top of the foot or hand, at the base of the toes or fingers, and this should be worked regularly. Since the endocrine system is of great significance in the reproductive system, all glands reflexes should receive some attention. Reflexological massage can also be used as a general technique to maintain healthy breasts. Essentially the hand should form a cup around the breast with the fingers underneath and the nipple between thumb and forefinger. Using a circular movement the breast is massaged slightly upwards. This should help retain the shape of the breast, and maintain its tone.

Diseases of the immune system

Antibodies and the lymphatic system

The human body resists infection by means of antibodies and white blood cells. Antibodies are protein substances, produced by the lymphoid tissue (spleen, thymus gland and the lymph nodes), that circulate in the blood. They react with their corresponding antigens (foreign bodies that cause antibodies to be formed) and make them harmless. There are a number of immunoglobulins (large protein molecules) that act as antibodies, and each has a particular function. For example, one is responsible for allergic reactions and another is produced to fight bacteria and viruses in the body.

The lymphatic system is also important in the body's immune response. Lymph nodes are swellings that occur at various points in the system. They are found in the neck, groin and armpit, and their main function is to remove foreign particles from the lymph and to participate in the immune response. In this latter function they become enlarged and produce lymphocytes, a type of white blood cell, which locate and neutralize antigens or produce antibodies, depending upon their type.

The lymph itself is a colourless, watery fluid. It is derived from blood and is similar to plasma. It contains 95 per cent water, with protein, sugar, salt and lymphocytes. It is circulated by muscular action and pumped through the lymph nodes for filtering.

It is clear that the lymphatic system and the immune system overall are very important in maintaining good health. Any disorder or deficiency in this system will lead to illness, which in some cases may be life-threatening. Reflexology may prove useful in restoring the balance although the need for professional medical advice should always be borne in mind.

Reflex points for the immune system

A number of reflexes for the lymph glands can be worked on the back of the hands, located over the wrists (*see* the diagrams on page 102) and on the top of the foot (*see* page 99). The spleen reflex is also an important one because the spleen itself produces lymphocytes (amongst other things). Associated reflexes that should be worked are those for the endocrine glands, circulation and liver.

In the case of infectious diseases, many of which occur in childhood (such as measles, mumps and chickenpox), the infection will normally run its course and as a result confer immunity to further bouts. To minimize discomfort and aid the recovery, the reflexes for the brain, solar plexus, circulation, endocrine glands and liver should be massaged.

The same applies to most infectious conditions, even autoimmune diseases where the antibodies attack their own body cells. Here, the lymph gland reflexes are particularly important.

Reiki

Introduction

A complementary therapy

Reiki is a method of natural healing that is centred upon 'universal life energy', the meaning of the Japanese word *reiki*. The therapy was named after Dr Mikao Usui, a Japanese theologist who rediscovered the art of healing, using and transferring this universal life energy. Following a prolonged period of meditation, Dr Usui acquired the ability of transferring reiki energy. He was also able to help others to act as channels for this energy.

To benefit fully from the technique, it is preferable to be initiated into the reiki energy. This is done by a reiki master. A number of reiki grand masters brought the practice to the West to allow many people to prepare themselves for self-discovery. reiki is now used to heal, either the practitioner or others, in meditation and in conjunction with other therapies such as aromatherapy.

In many cases traditional reiki, as generated by Dr Usui, forms the basis of reiki-do, an amplification of the technique which essentially translates into using reiki as a way of life. This aspect of reiki will be discussed more fully in due course.

Reiki energy

Reiki energy is regarded as life energy at its most effective—with the maximum vibration. It is considered to have an almost divine quality and as such includes everything in a world where problems and disorders are deemed to be caused by the feeling of detachment from the world. There is no division of reiki energy into positive and negative forms, but when people undergo a session of therapy, they allow the energy to be taken into themselves with beneficial effects. Essentially, those receiving reiki energy decide subconsciously just how much of the life energy is taken in.

Those who use reiki regularly often find that they are more joyful and lively and that their own inbuilt energy is enhanced—almost as if their batteries had been fully charged. Existing conflicts within the person are broken down and there is a greater vitality, leading to relaxation and a stimulation of the body. As this improvement develops, the natural processes of renewal and removal of toxins are enhanced and rendered more effective, ultimately opening up more of the body to the life energy.

Body organs such as the skin and protective systems such as the immune system are improved, providing the individual is prepared to undertake reiki regularly and in the first place to undergo an attunement or initiation into reiki energy. The initiation is merely a means whereby the universal life energy is bestowed through the reiki master. The reiki master acts as a channel and a link to release the healing power in the individual.

An initiation is not absolutely essential but it allows the individual access to the universal life energy that is used rather than his or her own life energy. Also, an initiation conveys a greater capacity for using reiki energy, with no associated tiredness, and, further, it provides a protective mechanism against any negative manifestations.

The treatment

Effects and limitations

There are several interrelated effects that result from taking in reiki energy:

- it enables the universal life energy to be received;
- it creates a feeling of deep relaxation;
- energy blockages are removed, allowing a flow of life energy throughout the body;
- toxins of various sorts are removed; these and other waste products are removed from the system much more quickly.

When the toxins have been removed from the body, more energy can be received and the vital processes and functions become more highly tuned. When the body takes in more and more life energy, it is said that its frequency becomes higher, facilitating contact with the Universal Spirit and generating trust in the universal life energy.

Deep relaxation is central to reiki therapy and is very much dependent upon the divine quality attributed to the energy. The extent to which reiki can work is defined by the receiver of the energy because only the necessary amount of energy is drawn in. A refusal to accept reiki, whether or not it is made consciously, will result in no energy flowing. This is, in a way, one limitation of reiki, albeit self-imposed. It should also be appreciated that attitude is very important and if someone attempts to use reiki in the wrong way, it will not work. Self-discovery must go hand in hand with everyday experience of real life. It is not possible to hide from the troubles of the real world through misplaced introspection.

A qualified therapist in the appropriate discipline must be sought to deal with major problems and difficulties. Of course, adopting reiki in tandem with another therapy will be very beneficial as the reiki will maximize the treatment being received.

The use of whole-body reiki

Because no one part of the body exists independently and because a disease or disorder in one area will inevitably affect the whole body, the use of reiki is best applied in a whole-body way to cleanse and revitalize the complete system.

Many practitioners undertake a particular routine before commencing a regime of whole-body treatment, and the main elements are briefly described below.

Preparing for whole-body reiki

It is a good idea to prepare thoroughly for reiki treatment to capitalize fully upon the beneficial effects. The following is a possible routine:

Remove jewellery

Most people wear jewellery of some description, whether stones of a semiprecious or precious nature, metal rings or chains, leather thongs or one of a whole variety of objects. Some metals and stones are believed to attract energies that may interfere with the life energy of reiki. Other items such as watches create a closed circuit that reduces the flow of life energy. In a way, items of jewellery can be seen as objects that create interference in the 'signal' in much the same way that an engine or motor can generate annoying interference in the reception of a radio programme. Earrings can also be a problem because in the case of pierced ears the earrings conflict with the flow of energy—the ear is very important in other therapies such as acupuncture and must therefore be kept unencumbered.

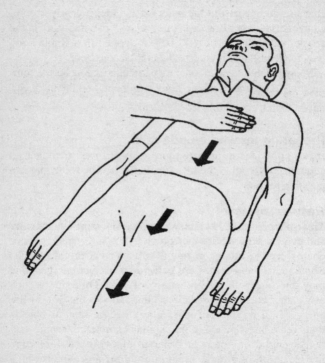

Even out the aura

Wash hands

The benefits of washing your hands are twofold. Firstly, there is the physical effect of cleaning, which has the additional quality of making the hands pleasant to feel for the recipient of reiki. It is essential that hot, sticky hands are not used in reiki as this would hardly be conducive to the state of relaxation being sought.

The second benefit relates to the aura surrounding the body. This aura may be affected by contact with objects, people, etc, over the course of the day and washing removes such influences, which could, in sensitive people, have an adverse effect.

Say a prayer

It is helpful at this stage to recite a short prayer asking for healing and to concentrate upon and acknowledge your aims, self-perception and those of the person upon whom your hands will be placed.

Even out the aura

This is a means of gently making contact and starting the therapy and may be carried out as follows:

- your partner/client/friend should lie down (*see* diagram on page 146);
- sitting at his or her side put your left hand on your sacrum (the five fused vertebrae in the lower part of the back);
- with your right hand held about 15–25 cm (6–9 inches) above the body and palm facing down, move your hand along the length of the body from the head to the toes;
- return the hand to the starting point, using a circular motion along the side of the body;
- repeat this three or four times.

This process can be repeated after the reiki therapy when your left hand can be placed on the sacrum of your partner/client/friend.

Energize

When each reiki therapy session is complete the whole body may be energized via the root chakra (*see* page 166 for chakras). The hand is held vertically above the body and then quickly moved from the pelvis to the head.

These preparatory rituals should be performed only when they are perceived to have some significance. There is little point going through the procedures if you do not see the reason why, but clearly some aspects of the procedure can be understood easily and will be accepted readily by the recipient.

The practicalities of whole-body reiki

Before the treatment

There is great scope for variation in the number and sequence of positions used for whole-body treatment. It will depend greatly upon the practitioner and what is felt to be best for the recipient, but no one sequence can be deemed the best one for all. It is important to be certain that your client/partner is not suffering from any illness or condition that might require the attention of another health professional. Reiki has its particular uses but it is unwise to try to address problems that clearly fall beyond its scope. The client can easily ask advice from his or her doctor, or other professional, as to whether they should undergo reiki therapy.

When it is clear that therapy can go ahead, the next commitment to be made is that of time. It is essential that both parties agree to pledge the time to make the most of the reiki therapy. It is likely that the practitioner will, in acting as a

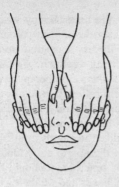

A—The basic position on the head

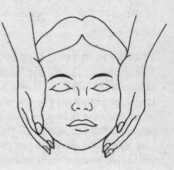

B—Alternative arrangement
on the head

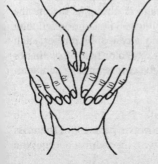

C—Hands on the back of the head

channel for the universal life energy, see his or her own status develop.

The extent of each session of reiki will vary depending upon circumstances and the individual receiving treatment. Certain positions may be better left out of the sequence or therapy may be focused on a particular area to help relieve blockages or deal with tension. If the recipient is currently on a regime of medication then a shorter session may be appropriate.

Similarly, if dealing with a small child or an elderly or infirm person, it is probably wise to limit the therapy to a session of 15 to 20 minutes. In all cases the reiki practitioner should be sensitive to and aware of the condition, needs and wellbeing of the recipient.

Positions in reiki therapy

The hands are clearly the 'instruments' of healing in reiki, and although the position in which they are placed on the recipient is meaningful, it may not be possible, nor is it essential, that the exact position is copied. Just placing the hands on the appropriate part of the body will suffice.

It should be pointed out that although the diagrams show unclothed bodies, reiki is usually carried out on a clothed recipient. reiki can be effected through clothing, as the energy will flow just as well. For partners, the reiki can be undertaken in the nude if wished. If there are any physical blemishes, such as a burn or other wound, the hands should be held a few inches above the skin at this area, around the corresponding acupuncture point or reflex zone.

The head

On the head, the basic position is shown on page 149. The hands are placed either side of the nose, with the palms covering the

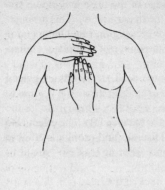

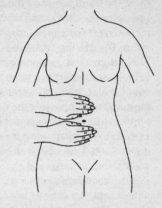

A—Arrangement for the thymus gland, heart and lungs

B—Arrangement for the stomach and digestive organs

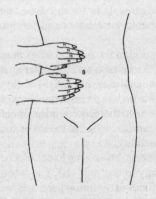

C—Focus on the gall bladder and liver

D—Focus on the appendix, intestines and urogenital organs

eyes; the thumbs rest by the bridge of the nose and the fingertips cover the cheeks and reach the upper lip (A). This arrangement covers the sinuses, eyes, pituitary gland and teeth and is
useful for dealing with colds, sinusitis, eye complaints, allergies, fatigue and general discontent.

In the second arrangement for the head, the hands are placed
over the ears, with the fingertips extending down the jawline to
the neck, encompassing the ears, of course, which includes the
semicircular canals responsible for balance (B). The effect also
extends to the pharyngeal area. Diseases and problems of these
organs—colds, trouble with balance, hearing loss, etc—are dealt
with in this arrangement.

If the hands are placed on the back of the head (C), this helps
with conditions such as headaches, colds, asthma and circulatory problems. It generally promotes relaxation.

The chest and abdomen

The next sequence of hand arrangements is for the chest and
abdomen. Once again there are many variations but a selection
is presented here.

The arrangement for the thymus gland, heart and lungs is as
follows: one hand is laid across the thymus and the other is at
90°, starting just below and between the breasts (A). The thymus is a bilobed gland in the neck which is an important part of
the immune system. This arrangement therefore reinforces the
immune system and helps the lymphatic system, the heart and
lungs and counters any general debility.

The next illustration in the sequence shows the hands placed
either side of the navel and slightly to one side (B). The stomach and digestive organs are the focus of attention here, and the
conditions/symptoms addressed necessarily have a link with
these body systems. As such this will help digestion and the

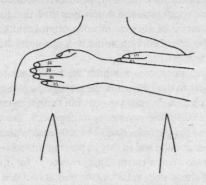

*A—Focus on the back to help lungs, heart,
muscular tension and headaches*

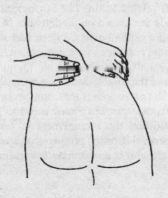

*B—Focus on the lower back to help
kidneys and adrenal glands*

metabolism in general terms and specifically will combat nausea, heartburn, gastrointestinal diseases and indigestion. Because the presence of such conditions often results in tension and worry, the relief of symptoms will similarly help relieve anxiety and depression.

Next are two positions in which the hands are placed in a position similar to that shown in the arrangement used to focus on the stomach and digestive organs but farther away from the body midline (C). One version is to approach the body from the right side of the partner/client. The left hand is placed around the base of the ribcage and in this way the gall bladder and liver are the organs to be dealt with. This position is for diseases and conditions of these important organs and associated problems of a metabolic nature. The liver is a vital organ in the process of removing toxins from the body and this arrangement can therefore be very important.

The position related to this one is essentially a reflection, where the hands are placed on the left side of the body to encompass the area of the bowels, spleen and some of the pancreas. Accordingly diseases of these organs, indigestion and healthy blood are all dealt with.

The position of the hands where the pelvic bones are covered and meet over the pubic area is for a number of ailments, many associated with the appendix, intestines and urinogenital organs (D). In addition, this arrangement is considered suitable for allergies, general debility, problems of a sexual nature and related to weight and is appropriate to reinforce the immune system.

The back

There are a number of arrangements that can be adopted on the back and lower back. The first diagram on page 153 shows one such position with a number of effects but it is likely that by gently experimenting a slightly different yet equally beneficial arrangement can be found. Here the hands are placed across the shoulder blades, at mid to upper point, to influence the intestines, lung, heart and various muscles in the neck and shoulder region (A). This will help lung and heart diseases, muscular tension, headaches and related conditions.

If the hands are placed lower down the back, around the midriff (on the lower ribs), this position will accommodate the kidneys and adrenal glands (B). (The adrenal glands are situated one each on the upper surface of each kidney and are important because they manufacture hormones that control a variety of body functions.)

In addition to these specific positions, there are many other reiki positions to deal with a multitude of complaints, and the reader is referred to a more extensive account for greater detail. It must always be remembered that serious conditions or diseases of a particular nature should be dealt with by the appropriate specialist.

The benefits of whole-body reiki

A reinforcing effect

It is believed with reiki, as with many similar forms of therapy, that the body cannot be treated in separate parts, as discrete organs that have little or nothing to do with other parts of the body. There are many conditions and diseases that affect the wellbeing of the individual as a whole or have a knock-on effect, even although the symptoms may be less tangible, such as anxiety or depression.

It is thus important that reiki is used not just to counteract a particular symptom but to treat the whole body to achieve the relaxation mentioned earlier and with it the removal of blockages in energy flow and the dispersal of toxins.

Long-term whole-body reiki should be adopted in all cases, and in a therapy session of 60 to 90 minutes all parts of the body will be addressed and receive reiki energy. Over a period of time, the general condition of the body is restored and the energy channels are opened to allow the body to deal properly and naturally with both stress and the buildup of toxins.

In cases of recovery from illness, reiki therapy provides the additional energy to bolster recovery and will reinforce the effects of any other method of natural healing. It can be used as a supplementary therapy almost as a general, ongoing policy as it is a truly complementary system of treatment.

Reduction of side-effects

It is well known that the use of drugs to combat, say, an infection may at first seem very effective. However, it is becoming all too obvious that the excessive use of drugs is causing its own problems. In the case of many drugs, uncomfortable, distressing and even threatening side effects can ensue. With antibiotics, there is now the problem of drug resistance in bacteria, leading to situations where hospital patients are vulnerable to infections from so-called superbugs or killer bugs. This has resulted specifically from the overuse of antibiotics and has reached the point where hospitals now have only one or two very powerful drugs to use in these circumstances.

Reiki therapy can be a very useful adjunct for anyone taking a course of drugs. It can help reduce some side effects and generally aid the body in recovery when the course has been completed. Postoperative recovery will benefit from reiki and it can also help after chemotherapy. In all these cases reiki therapy supplies that extra life energy, enabling the body to bounce back more quickly from the burdens of surgery and chemicals.

In some cases, use of reiki therapy after an operation will lessen pain and the natural healing processes will be accelerated. The key in all these examples is that the reiki therapy must be undertaken on a regular basis. The added benefit of this is that when a person is enjoying good health, the regular therapy increases the body's inbuilt defences, which manifests itself as confidence and outward harmony in dealing with everyday events. It also bestows a greater ability to deal with stressful situations. This very positive outlook can become possible because once the blockages and toxins have been removed from the system, the scope for personal advancement and growth becomes available. In general, the better metabolic functioning afforded by reiki therapy means that benefits and improvements may be experienced in many ways.

Reiki associations

It has already been mentioned that reiki therapy can be undertaken in conjunction with other methods of natural healing. In addition, it can be combined with activities such as meditation and crystal therapy. The following sections consider briefly a few of these combinations, which for the present purpose have been called associations.

Reiki and the use of crystals

Crystal therapy is known to many people and involves the use of precious and semiprecious stones. The stones are thought to hold positive energy and they act as a conduit for healing from the practitioner to the recipient. It is also said that the stones generate a healing vibration that acts upon the body. In some cases the stone is placed on the body where treatment is focused, in others it may be positioned on the appropriate acupuncture point. Most therapists use quartz for physical healing, amethyst for spiritual healing and rose quartz to heal emotions. Fluorite may also be used to develop awareness and knowledge of a spiritual nature.

In reiki, three varieties of quartz are commonly used—amethyst, rose quartz and ordinary quartz (or rock crystal). The crystal structure of quartz is often taken to be related to the six chakras and the tip of the crystal to the seventh chakra. Practitioners recommend using rock crystal to avoid feeling overpowered by changes, mounting pressures and the stress of everyday life. Carrying the crystal or wearing it is meant to bring light into your workaday routines.

Rock crystal can also be used in conjunction with reiki meditation (of which see later), being held between, or in, the hands. In this way the energy emanating from the crystal is thought to go into the palms and then the rest of the body via the reflex zones. It is recommended by some in a variety of applications, such as relaxation, wound-healing with other therapy and treating particular organs.

Rose quartz, with its soft pink coloration, is used for mending emotional problems. This may be dealing with problematic emotions, such as shutting out certain desires, or it may be facing trauma and stress brought about by a separation.

The use of amethyst with reiki is varied. It can help promote the proper function of an organ that has been under treatment. Placed on the third eye (the centre of the forehead) it facilitates clearer vision in one's path through life, and it can reduce tension and fear.

Meditation with reiki

Meditation in its own right is a useful therapy. It needs concentration and time and a will to continue with the practice. Some of the benefits may happen straight away (such as a lowering of the blood pressure) while others require some proficiency. It has been reported that it helps with insomnia, and high blood pressure can be lowered significantly, enough to allow dependence on drugs to be reduced. Meditation is undertaken in a quiet room and it must be done at least half an hour after consuming food or drink. When a person is sitting comfortably, the mind is then concentrated upon excluding the hustle and bustle, problems, tension and overstimulating thoughts of modern life.

Reiki assists in this concentration, with the flow of energy aiding relaxation. There are some positions that can be adopted in reiki meditation to achieve particular goals. In the first position the legs are drawn up and the soles of the feet put together with the knees falling apart. This can be done while lying down or sitting against a wall or chair. The hands adopt a praying gesture. This is meant to complete the circuit of energy, allowing a flow around the body. The reiki energy removes any blockages, and, when performed regularly, this becomes a powerful meditation exercise. It can be done for short periods initially, just a couple of minutes, and then built up gradually in small increases.

To achieve complete harmony with your partner, there is a meditation exercise that can be done together. Sitting facing each other, the legs are spread, with the knees raised slightly. Moving closer, the legs of one are put over the legs of the partner and palms are put together. This allows a joint circuit of energy which strengthens the harmonious and loving relationship between two people. Done properly, this meditation may take up to half an hour.

Group meditation is also possible with reiki, in which the participants stand in a circle with hands joined.

Aromatherapy blended with reiki

Aromatherapy is considered elsewhere in this volume (*see* page 211). It is essentially a healing method that employs essential oils extracted from plants, usually in a neutral oil base (carrier oil). The oils can be used in three ways: by direct application, bathing in water to which a few drops of the appropriate oil have been added, and inhalation.

When used in conjunction with reiki, some oils can be applied directly on particular areas of the body, or their aroma can be made to fill the room using an aroma lamp. Below a few oils are considered and their use compared to their therapeutic value in aromatherapy. It is very likely that someone with a knowledge of essential oils will be able to capitalize upon their experience and incorporate further oils in their reiki therapy.

- *Lavender*—in aromatherapy lavender is a tonic with relaxing effects. It is also antiseptic, an antispasmodic and stimulates the appetite. It is a widely used and versatile oil that is used for minor burns and wounds. Its soothing effects render it helpful for headaches, tension and similar conditions.

  In reiki, lavender is associated primarily with patients/recipients who are sensitive and easily hurt, essentially introverts. It can be used in long sessions of reiki when the lavender helps to promote the calm and confidence necessary for a period of building and strengthening of the life force energy.

- *Sandalwood*—this oil is used in aromatherapy for its relaxing and antiseptic effects. It forms a very effective oil for application to the skin (especially facial), particularly for dry or sensitive skin.

  The use of sandalwood in reiki therapy is quite different.

Its benefit seems to be in producing an ambience conducive to the reiki therapy itself because the oil is considered to elicit trust and confidence between practitioner and recipient.

- *Clary sage*—this is a very useful oil with a number of qualities including those of being tonic, antispasmodic, antidepressant, anti-inflammatory, bactericidal and more. It is also used to treat colds and menstrual problems and its very low toxicity renders it suitable for general use.

  In a session of reiki therapy, clary sage has been used to open blocked channels and to enhance sensitivity.

- *Patchouli*—apart from being accredited with some aphrodisiac qualities, patchouli is more commonly used in aromatherapy to treat skin disorders and minor burns because of its anti-inflammatory and antiseptic qualities.

  While patchouli is also used in reiki therapy for allergies and impurities of the skin, the fundamental use and aim is to enhance the sensual qualities and aspects of life.

Other reiki associations

Because reiki is very much a positive therapy and benign, it can be undertaken in conjunction with other therapies with no harm. However, there are some beneficial effects of reiki that may affect in some way the activity of other courses of treatment.

- *Prescription drugs*—many reiki therapists believe that reiki can readily affect the way in which such drugs work in the body. It has already been mentioned that side effects of drugs can be lessened through the use of reiki, and in some cases it is reported that the drug's process will be accelerated. In addition, reiki makes the body more receptive and therefore therapy prior to the course of a drug may enhance its effect.

The relaxed state engendered by reiki may also counter, to some extent, the efficacy of an anaesthetic. However, injections such as anaesthetics can more readily and easily be released from the body with the help of reiki.

Although minor pains can often be remedied through the use of reiki alone, stronger painkillers do not have their effect lessened by reiki. The interaction between reiki and drugs is neither well tested nor documented, but the overall positive effect of the therapy means that it is not likely to cause any problems.

- *Homeopathy*—in conjunction with this therapy, reiki provides a reinforcing effect by rendering the treatment more effective. reiki can help avoid strain, improve the removal of toxins and increase the body's sensitivity. After treatment, whole-body reiki will help recovery.
- *Bach remedies*—these are named after Edward Bach, an English doctor who in the early years of the 19th century gave up his Harley Street practice to concentrate upon finding plants with healing qualities. He identified 38 plants, the flowers of which he floated on clear spring water. This, he believed, transferred medicinal properties to the water, which could then be given to patients. This practice he developed to mimic the drops of dew on the plant, which in the first instance were used. Intended for home self-help, the remedies are meant for treating the whole person. Stock solutions are diluted in water and a few drops taken.

Typical examples are:

  - cherry plum for fear, tension, irrationality
  - holly for envy, jealousy and hatred
  - pine for guilt and constantly apologizing
  - sweet chestnut for despair
  - wild rose for apathy

In common with many other examples, reiki improves the effectiveness of Bach remedies.

Determining the need

Introduction

When undertaking reiki therapy it is often necessary to determine the need for therapy in the client or partner. As therapists work with reiki for longer, they become more sensitive and proficient and are better able to judge problem areas on what is called the subtle plane (the etheric body). Expertise comes only with experience, but it seems that there are certain reactions or feelings detected that may be indicative. Before trying to perceive a person's need, some practitioners 'sensitize' their hands. This involves holding the palms facing, about 40 to 50 cm (15 to 20 in) apart and slowly bringing them together. The movement should be spread out over four or five minutes to allow an attunement and for changes to be perceived.

The following are some possible responses that may be experienced:

- *Attraction*—implies that reiki energy is needed at that point.
- *Repulsion*—suggests a long-established blockage is present that is restricting the flow of energy. This may require a considerable period of therapy to rectify.
- *Flow*—a positive feeling representing the flow of life energy which will be enhanced by further reiki energy, raising the entire system.
- *Heat*—if your hands feel warmer, it signifies a need for life energy. If the whole body produces such a result, reiki energy can be applied anywhere.
- *Cold*—this is probably because of a blockage in energy flow

such that an area of the body has been deprived of energy. Such blockages may also require considerable attention and both whole-body and specific treatment will probably be required.

- *Tingling*—an inflamed area will usually produce a tingling in the hands of the therapist. The strength of the stimulus reflects the severity of the problem and additional help from a medical practitioner may be identified as being necessary.
- *Pain*—this usually represents a buildup of energy in some form. A sharp pain reflects that the energy is beginning to dissipate and in so doing is causing some conflict elsewhere in the system. In this case, whole-body therapy is beneficial before concentrating upon a particular area.

There are other methods to determine need and to identify disruptions in the flow of life energy, but these are, in the main, for the more experienced practitioner. However, details can be found in a variety of publications and involve pendulum dowsing, activity of the chakras and the use of systems such as the tarot or the I Ching. These latter two, however, are not for novices.

When the need is answered

If reiki is practised regularly, it can have a very positive effect and influence. One of the major problems with modern life is the very pace of life itself—every day seems to be hectic, full of demands and pressure which result in stress, discomfort and ragged emotions.

These emotional ups and downs and stressful pressures are smoothed out by reiki. A more balanced approach to life is developed; a greater inner harmony is achieved, which means that the quality of life improves and any illnesses or condition become less of a problem, responding more readily to treatment or cleared up seemingly of their own accord. The flow of energy from reiki ensures that there is harmony between the third eye (which identifies the ideal path for the individual) and the root chakra (or energy centre). (For an explanation of the chakras *see* page 166.)

The significance of chakras with reiki

Chakras are a common concept in several disciplines of alternative medicine or traditional Asian medicine. A chakra is a centre of energy, subtle energy in reiki, which has several functions. In addition to being 'representative' of a particular organ or group of organs, a chakra also controls our being on different levels and it links these two representative states.

The chakras

In reiki there are considered to be seven major and a number of minor chakras. The seven major chakras are shown in the diagram on page 166. These are, from the lowest to the highest: the root chakra, the sexual chakra, the personality chakra, the heart chakra, the expressive chakra, the knowledge chakra and the crown chakra.

The number of major chakras does vary in some instances, e.g. Hindu yoga has six centres, but the greatest variation is in the minor chakras. In some regimes of therapy ten minor chakras are identified, and these are interconnected with the major chakras. A typical system could be:

- one in the arch of each foot, connected to the first and third chakras (root and personality);
- one in each knee joint, connected to the fifth and sixth chakras (expressive and knowledge);
- one in each palm, connected to the second, third and fourth chakras (sexual, personality and heart);

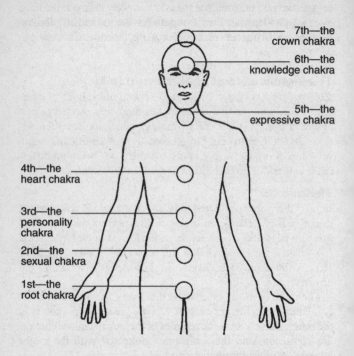

7th—the
crown chakra

6th—the
knowledge chakra

5th—the
expressive chakra

4th—the
heart chakra

3rd—the
personality
chakra

2nd—the
sexual chakra

1st—the
root chakra

The seven major chakras

- one in each elbow, connected to the second and third chakras (sexual and personality);
- one below each shoulder, connected to the third and fifth chakras (personality and expressive).

Brief summaries of the major chakras are given below, followed by an indication of how the chakras interact with reiki.

The root or base chakra

This is the source of strength and is essential for proper development. The other centres of energy rely upon the root chakra to perform properly. Disorders within the root chakras may result in mental problems (e.g. aggression, confusion) or physical symptoms (e.g. of the intestines, excretory systems or bones).

The sexual or sacral chakra

This is highly influential and governs sensual and sexual factors, the means whereby experiences are felt and registered. Blockages result in a variety of phobias or conditions, such as a fear of being touched, general incomprehension or obsessive cleanliness. Physical manifestations may include being prone to infections or problems with the kidneys/bladder or lymphatic system.

The personality or solar plexus chakra

This is the power centre and focus of personal freedom or, conversely, feelings of guilt. Mental consequences of a blockage might be anxiety about how others perceive one, envy or selfish greed. Physically there could be digestive disorders, liver and gall bladder problems or disorders of the pancreas.

The heart chakra

This effectively controls self-acceptance and by extension everyone else around us. Blockages may result in attitudes such as selfishness or emotional blackmail. Physical manifestations could be disorders of the lungs and heart, and circulatory problems.

The expressive or throat chakra

The expressive chakra controls overall self-expression, whether it is in language or gesture. An upset in this centre could well result in an individual becoming dictatorial while the physical signs could be growth problems or a muscular tension leading to a lack of vocal control.

The knowledge or brow chakra

Otherwise known as the third eye, this is the focus of intuition, the perception of truth, which enables a person to find his or her own course through life. Accordingly, a blockage of this chakra will culminate in a haphazard approach to life and probably an inability to settle down to any one task for any length of time.

The crown chakra

It is generally felt that the seventh, crown, chakra is appreciated only by experience and it depends upon the other six for its development.

The practicalities of chakras with reiki

This is quite a complicated aspect of reiki, and to develop it as an integral part of a programme of reiki, the reader should seek a more extensive treatment of the subject. Some information is, however, presented here by way of an introduction.

Some therapists use the technique of balancing chakras to attune completely the energy on the subtle plane. The chakras are paired, first with sixth (root with knowledge), second with fifth (sexual with expressive) and third with fourth (personality with heart) by placing the hands on the relevant areas. When it feels through the hands as if the energy is balanced with the first and sixth chakras, then the second and fifth can be balanced in the same way. Other combinations may be used if it is felt that these may be beneficial.

The chakras may suffer a number of problems, creating an imbalance, and although considerable corrective therapy may be required, a balance can be achieved with reiki. Many practitioners recommend sending reiki energy through a problematic chakra. This involves placing one hand at the front of the body, above the chakra, and the other hand at the back of the body. The flow of universal life energy eventually corrects any defects. However, it is important to remember that because of the interconnection of the chakras, defects in one affect the whole system. Therefore the healing cannot be undertaken in isolation. It is always good practice to balance the chakras after a session of specific healing.

Higher levels of reiki

Although it is possible to progress beyond the level of proficiency implied so far, second and third degree reiki are really for the experts. This is particularly so with third degree reiki, the details of which are not written down.

Available power is increased with second degree reiki but should only be accessed by someone working with a reiki master. The greater flow of energy means that the effect of reiki therapy is greater and also that its effect on a mental and emotional level is enhanced. Further, it is said that reiki at this level can be transmitted over distances, to one or a number of people. This is, of course, highly specialized and advice should be sought from a reiki master by anyone wishing to pursue this goal.

Reiki-do

In Japanese, *do* means 'path', hence reiki-do is concerned with a way of life in which reiki figures very prominently. Reiki-do is, of course, founded on the reiki therapy described in the preceding pages and it consists of three aspects that enable personal growth. The three categories of reiki-do are:

- *Inner*—based upon meditation, as described earlier, and can be augmented by one of the methods outlined, such as the scents of aromatherapy. It adopts a whole-body system of treatment, leading to a greater awareness and vitality.
- *Outer*—the application of reiki energy forms the basis of this part of reiki-do, with the chakras, crystals and other subsidiary therapies.
- *Synergistic*—as the word implies, this is the combination of parts which have, when used together, a greater effect than their combined individual effects, that is, a merger of inner and outer reiki-do which exceeds the anticipated combined effect. It is particularly appropriate for anyone who has reasonable experience in this therapy and can appreciate the nonexclusive nature of pleasure and success.

Conclusions

Reiki is a technique of healing available to anyone. It can lead to a more relaxed approach to life and greater harmony with the total environment. It can also be applied to plants and animals, for example your household pets, and for this and further information about the therapy, the reader is advised to seek more detailed treatments.

Shiatsu

Introduction

Origins

Shiatsu originated in China at least 2000 years ago, when the earliest accounts gave the causes of ailments and the remedies that could be effected through a change of diet and way of life. The use of massage and acupuncture was also recommended. The Japanese also practised this massage, after it had been introduced into their country, and it was known as *anma*. The therapy that is known today as *shiatsu* has gradually evolved with time from anma under influences from both East and West. It is only very recently that it has gained recognition and popularity, with people becoming aware of its existence and benefits.

Although East and West have different viewpoints on health and life, these can complement one another. The Eastern belief is of a primary flow of energy throughout the body, which runs along certain channels known as meridians. It is also believed that this energy exists throughout the universe and that all living creatures are dependent upon it as much as on physical nourishment. The energy is known by three similar names, *ki*, *chi* and *prana* in Japan, China and India respectively, with the chi form now widely used in the West. (It should be noted that the term 'energy' in this context is not the same as the physical quantity that is measured in joules or calories.) As in acupuncture, there are certain pressure points on the meridians that relate to certain organs, and these points are known as *tsubos*.

The applications of shiatsu

Shiatsu can be used to treat a variety of minor problems, such as insomnia, headaches, anxiety, back pain, etc. Western medicine may be unable to find a physical cause for a problem, and although some pain relief may be provided, the underlying cause of the problem may not be cured. It is possible that one session of shiatsu will be sufficient to remedy the problem by stimulating the flow of energy along the channels. A regime of exercise (possibly a specific routine) with a change in diet and/or lifestyle may also be recommended. Shiatsu can encourage a general feeling of good health in the whole person, not just in the physical sense. After some study or practice, shiatsu can be performed on friends and relatives. There are many benefits for both the giver and the receiver of shiatsu, both on a physical and spiritual level.

Energy or chi

Auras

There are believed to be a number of *auras*, or energy layers, that surround the physical body and can be detected or appreciated (*see* the figure on page 173). The first layer, the *etheric body*, is the most dense and is connected with the body and the way it works. An exercise is described later that enables this layer to be detected. The *astral body* is much wider, is affected by people's feelings and, if viewed by a clairvoyant, is said to change in colour and shape depending on the feelings being experienced. The next aura is the *mental body*, which is involved with the thought processes and intelligence of a person. Similarly, this can be viewed by a clairvoyant and is said to contain 'pictures' of ideas emanating from the person. These first three auras comprise the personality of a person. The last

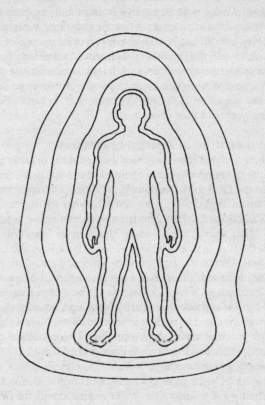

Auras

aura is known as the *causal body*, *soul* or *higher self*. This is concerned more with perceptive feelings and comprehension. It is believed in reincarnation that the first three auras die with the body, but the causal body carries on in its process of development by adopting another personality. As a person grows in maturity and awareness, these different auras are used and energy is passed from one layer to another. It therefore follows that any alteration in the physical state will, in turn, affect the other layers, and vice versa.

Seven centres of energy, or chakras

It is believed that there are seven main *chakras* (a chakra being a centre of energy) found in a midline down the body, from the top of the head to the bottom of the torso (*see* figure on page 166, under Reiki) . They are situated along the *sushumna*, or spiritual channel, which runs from the crown of the head to the base of the trunk. Energy enters the channel from both ends. Since the flow is most efficient when the back is straight, this is the ideal posture for meditation or when powers of concentration are required. Each chakra has a component of each aura, and it comprises what is known as a centre of consciousness. Each aura is activated as a person develops, and the same occurs with the chakras, beginning with the lowest (the root chakra) and progressing to the others with time. There is also a change of energy between the auras of each chakra.

Shiatsu associates the crown chakra with the pineal gland, which controls the right eye and upper brain and affects spiritual matters. The knowledge chakra is linked with the pituitary gland, which controls the left eye, lower brain, nose and nervous system. It has an effect on the intellect, perception, intuition and comprehension. The expressive chakra is concerned with the thyroid gland and governs the lymphatic system, hands, arms, shoulders, mouth, vocal cords, lungs and throat. It affects communication, creativity and self-expression. The heart chakra is concerned with the thymus gland and controls the heart, breasts, vagus nerve and circulatory system, and affects self-awareness, love, humanitarian acts and compassion. The personality chakra is concerned with the pancreas. It controls the spleen, gall bladder, liver and digestive system and stomach and has an effect on desire, personal power and the origin of emotions. The sexual chakra affects the gonads and controls the lower back, feet, legs and reproductive system. This affects physical, sexual and mental energy, relationships and self-worth. The root chakra is concerned with the adrenal glands. It controls the skeleton, parasympathetic and sympathetic nervous systems, bladder and kidneys, and affects reproduction and the physical will. As an example of this, if a person is suffering from an ailment of the throat, it is possible that he or she may also be unable to voice private thoughts and feelings.

Zang and fu organs

Energy storage and production

According to traditional Eastern therapies, organs have a dual function—their physical one and another that is concerned with the use of energy and that might be termed an 'energetic function'. The twelve organs mentioned in the traditional therapies are split into two groups known as *zang* and *fu*, and each is described below.

Zang organs are for energy storage, and the fu organs produce energy from sustenance and drink and also control excretion. The organs can be listed in pairs, each zang matched by a fu with a similar function. Although the pancreas is not specifically mentioned, it is usually included with the spleen. The same applies to the 'triple heater' or 'triple burner', which is connected with the solar plexus, lower abdomen and the thorax. The lungs are a zang organ and are concerned with assimilation of energy, or chi, from the air, which with energy from food ensures the complete body is fed and that mental alertness and a positive attitude are maintained. This is paired with the fu organ of the large intestine, which takes sustenance from the small intestine, absorbs necessary liquids and excretes waste material via the faeces. It is also concerned with self-confidence. The spleen is a zang organ and changes energy or chi from food into energy that is needed by the body. It is concerned with the mental functions of concentration, thinking and analysing. This is paired with the fu organ of the stomach, which prepares food so that nutrients can be extracted and also any energy, or chi, can be taken. It also provides 'food for thought'. The zang organ of the heart assists blood formation from chi and controls the flow of blood and the blood vessels. It is where the mind is housed and therefore affects awareness, belief, long-term memory and feelings. This is paired with the fu organ of the small intestine, which divides food into necessary and unnecessary parts, the latter passing to the large intestine. It is also concerned with the making of decisions. The kidneys are a zang organ and they produce basic energy, or chi, for the other five paired organs and also for reproduction, birth, development and maturity. They also sustain the skeleton and brain and provide willpower and 'get up and go'. They are paired with the fu organ of the bladder, which stores waste fluids until they are passed as urine and also gives strength or courage. The zang organ of the 'heart governor' is concerned with the flow of blood throughout the body. It is a protector and help for the heart and has a bearing on relationships with other people. (Although there is no organ known as the 'heart governor', it is connected with the heart and its functions.) This is paired with the 'triple heater' or 'burner', which passes chi around the body and allows an emotional exchange with others. The liver is the sixth zang organ, and it assists with a regular flow of chi to achieve the most favourable physiological effects and emotional calmness. Positive feelings, humour, planning and creativity are also connected with it. The gall bladder is the sixth fu organ, with which the liver is paired, and this keeps bile from the liver and passes it to the intestines. It concerns decision-making and forward thinking.

The meridian system

The meridians, as previously mentioned, are a system of invisible channels on the back and front of the body along which energy, or chi, flows. There are twelve principal meridians plus two additional ones, which are called *the governing vessel* and the *conception* or *directing vessel*. Each meridian passes partly through the body and partly along the skin, joining various chakras and organs (the organs as recognized in traditional Eastern medicine). One end of every meridian is beneath the skin while the other is on the surface of the skin on the feet or hands. Along each meridian are acupressure or acupuncture points, which in shiatsu are called *tsubos*. These points allow the flow of energy along the meridian to be altered if necessary (*see* the figures on page 178). The meridians receive energy from the chakras and organs (as described previously), from the meridians with ends located on the feet and hands and also via the pressure points, or tsubos. Energy, or chi, can pass from one meridian into another as there is a 'pathway' linking each meridian to two others. The energy passes in a continuous cycle or flow and in a set order from one meridian to another. By working on the meridians, and particularly the pressure points, a

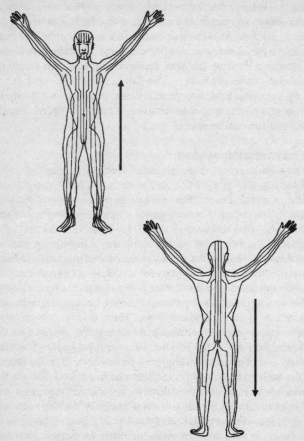

The flow of energy along the meridians

number of beneficial effects can be achieved with problems such as muscle tension, backache and headache. Since the flow of energy is stimulated by working on the meridians this will in turn affect the joints, muscles and skin and thereby ease these complaints. Since a person's mental state, feelings and moods are also altered by the flow of energy, this can induce a more positive frame of mind.

A person in good health should have a constant flow of chi, with no concentrations or imbalances in any part of the body. It is believed that the greater the amount of chi there is within a person's body, the greater the vitality, mental alertness and overall awareness that person will possess.

Feeling chi

It is possible for a person to 'feel' chi, and the following exercise helps demonstrate what it is like. Stand upright with the feet apart and the arms stretched upwards. Rub the hands together as if they were very cold, so that a feeling of warmth is generated. The backs of the hands, wrists and forearms should also be rubbed. The arms should be put down at the side of the body and shaken vigorously. This should then be repeated from the beginning, with the arms above the head and concluding with the shaking. Then hold the hands out to the front—they should have a pleasant feeling of warmth and vitality, which is due to the circulation of blood and energy that has been generated. The hands should be placed to the sides, then, after inhaling deeply, concentrate on relaxing as you exhale. This procedure should be done several times, and then it should be possible to feel the chi. The hands should be placed about 1 metre (3 feet) apart, with the palms of the hands facing inwards. After relaxation, concentrate your thoughts on the gap between your hands and then gradually reduce the space between them—but

Feeling chi

they must not touch. It is likely that when the hands come quite close, about 15–30 cm (6–12 in), a feeling of tingling or warmth may be felt or the sensation that there is something between the hands. This will be when the auras that surround the hands touch. To reinforce the sensation, the hands should be taken apart again and then closed together so that the feeling is experienced again and becomes more familiar.

The following exercise also enables chi to be felt, but this time it is the etheric aura around another person's head and shoulders. The previous procedure to generate chi should be repeated, but this time the hand should be placed near to another person's head, within 60 centimetres–1 metre (2–3 feet). This person should be sitting upright on the floor or on a chair. The hand should be moved gradually nearer to the seated person's head, concentrating attention on the gap between your hand and his or her head. If no sensation is felt, the hand should be moved back to its original position and the process should be repeated. Again, a feeling of tingling or warmth will probably be experienced as the person's aura is felt. When this has been achieved, the hand can progress round the head and down to the shoulders, noting the edge of the aura at the same time. If the person has no success in experiencing the aura, it is likely that the mind is not clear of other thoughts, so relaxation is suggested prior to any further attempt.

It is also possible for a person, by concentrating his or her thoughts and by a slight change of position, to alter the flow of chi in the body. This will have the effect of either making him or her feel a lot heavier or lighter, depending on which is desired. Taken to extremes, someone who is skilled at the control of chi will prove too heavy to be lifted by four people.

Basic rules

There are some basic rules that should be followed before the practice of shiatsu. Clothing should be comfortable, loose-fitting and made of natural fibres since this will help with the flow of energy or chi. The room should be warm, quiet, have adequate space and be neat and clean. If not, this can have an adverse effect on the flow of chi. The person receiving the therapy should ideally lie on a futon (a quilted Japanese mattress) or similar mat on the floor. If necessary, pillows or cushions should be ready to hand if the person does not feel comfortable. Shiatsu should not be given or received by someone who has just eaten a large meal—it is advisable to delay for several hours. No pressure should be exerted on varicose veins or injuries such as cuts or breaks in bones. Although shiatsu can be of benefit to women while pregnant, there are four areas that should be avoided. These are the stomach, any part of the legs from the knees downwards, the fleshy web of skin between the forefinger and thumb, and an area on the shoulders at each side of the neck. Ensure that the person is calm and relaxed. It is generally not advisable to practise shiatsu on people who have serious illnesses such as heart disorders, multiple sclerosis or cancer. An experienced practitioner may be able to help, but a detailed and accurate diagnosis and course of treatment is essential. A verbal check on the person's overall health is important and also to ascertain if a woman is pregnant. If there is any worry or doubt about proceeding, then the safest option is not to go ahead.

Although the general feeling after receiving shiatsu is one of wellbeing and relaxation, there are occasionally unpleasant results, such as coughing, generation of mucus or symptoms of a cold, a feeling of tiredness, a headache or other pains and aches, or feeling emotional. The coughing and production of mucus is because the body is being encouraged to rid itself of its surplus foods (such as sugars and fats) in this form. A cold can sometimes develop when the mucus is produced, usually when the cells of the body are not healthy. Tiredness can occur, frequently with a person who suffers from nervous tension. After therapy has removed this stress or tension, then the body's need for sleep and rest becomes apparent. A short-lived headache or other pain may also develop, for which there are two main reasons. Since shiatsu redresses the balance of chi in the body, this means that blockages in the flow of energy are released and the chi can rush around the body, causing a temporary imbalance in one part and resulting in an ache or pain. It is also possible that too much time or pressure may have been applied to a particular area. The amount needed varies considerably from one person to another. If a pain or headache is still present after a few days, however, it is sensible to obtain qualified medical help. Emotional feelings can occur while the energy is being stimulated to flow and balance is regained. The feelings may be connected with something from the past that has been suppressed and so, when these emotions resurface, it is best for them to be expressed in a way that is beneficial, such as crying. There may, of course, be no reaction at all. Some people are completely 'out of touch' with their bodies and are aware only that all is not well when pain is felt. If this is so, then any beneficial effects from shiatsu may not register. Because of a modern diet that contains an abundance of animal fats, people become overweight through the deposition of fat below the skin and around the internal organs. The body is unable to 'burn off' this fat, and this layer forms a barrier to chi. The flow is stopped, and overweight people do not tend to benefit as much because of the difficulty in stimulating the flow of chi in the body.

Exercises and the three main centres

The body is divided into three main centres—the head, the heart and the abdominal centres. The head centre is concerned with activities of a mental nature, such as imaginative and intellectual thought processes, and is concerned with the knowledge chakra. The heart centre is concerned with interactions among people and to the world in general, including the natural world. It is related to the expressive chakra and the heart chakra. The abdominal centre is related to the root, sexual and personality chakras and is concerned with the practical aspects of life and physical activity. Ideally, energy should be divided equally among the three but because of a number of factors, such as activity, education, diet, culture, etc, this is frequently not so. In shiatsu, more importance is attached to the abdominal centre, known as the *hara*. The following exercise uses abdominal breathing and, by so doing, not only is oxygen inhaled but also chi is taken into the hara where it increases a person's vitality.

Once the technique is mastered, it can be practised virtually anywhere and will restore composure and calmness.

Sit on the floor with the back straight and, if possible, in the position known in Japan as *seiza* (*see* diagram on page 185). The hands should be placed loosely together in the lap and the mind and body should become relaxed after some deep breathing. One hand should be put on the stomach, below the navel, and the other on the chest. When inhaling, this should not be done with the chest but with the abdomen, which should increase in size. As the person exhales the abdomen should contract, and this procedure should be practised for a few minutes. After a rest it should be repeated, inhaling quite deeply but still the chest should not be allowed to rise. Some people may not find this exercise at all difficult while others may need more practice. It may be that there is stress or tension in the diaphragm. Once the technique has been mastered and the hands do not need to be placed on the chest and abdomen, imagine that chi is being inhaled down into the hara. Sit in the same position and inhale slowly via the nose and imagine the chi descending (*see* figure on page 185). (It may aid concentration if the eyes are closed.) The breath should be held for about four seconds and concentration should be centred on the chi. Then exhale gradually through the mouth and repeat the process for a few minutes.

The next exercise is known as a centred movement, which practises movement of the chi, since it is one person's chi that should have an effect on another. After practising shiatsu on a partner, you should not feel tired but refreshed and exhilarated. This is a benefit of the extra chi in the body. The exercise should be begun on hands and knees (a body width apart), and it is most important that you are relaxed and comfortable with no tension. This position is the basis for other movements that are

Seiza

Inhaling through the nose

practised on others. While the position is maintained, begin to move the body backwards and forwards so that you are conscious of the transfer of weight, either on to the hands or knees. The body should then be moved slowly in a circular way, again being aware of the shift of weight from the hands, to hands and knees, to knees, etc, returning to the original position. You should also realize that as the whole body is moved, the abdomen is its 'centre of gravity'. Practise maintaining a position for about five seconds, registering the increase in weight on the hands when you move forwards and the reduction when you rock backwards. Then return to the original position. It is important that the body weight is always used at right angles to the receiver as this will have the maximum effect on the flow of chi. The reason for holding a particular position is that this has the effect of making the person's chi move.

The centred movement previously described can be practised on a partner in exactly the same way, following the same rules. The right hand should be placed on the sacrum, which is between the hips, and the left hand midway between the shoulder blades. As before, you should rock forwards and hold the position for about five seconds and then repeat after rocking backwards on to the knees (*see* the diagram on page 187). This basic procedure can be repeated about twelve times, and if you are not sure whether too much or too little pressure is being used, check with your partner. You will eventually acquire the skill of knowing what amount is right for a particular person.

To summarize, there are some basic rules to be followed when practising shiatsu. A person should make use of body weight and not muscular strength, and there should be no effort involved. At all times a calm and relaxed state should be maintained, and the weight of the body should be at right angles in relation to the receiver's body. The person's whole body should

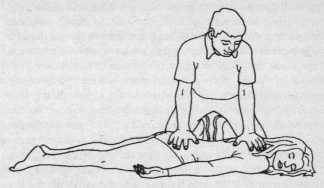

A centred movement

be moved when altering weight on to the receiver, maintaining the hara as the centre. Any weight or pressure held should be for a short time only and both hands should be used equally. It is best to maintain a regular pattern of movement while giving shiatsu, and always keep in physical contact with the receiver by keeping a hand on him or her throughout the therapy.

Shiatsu on the face and head

There are a large number of different exercises and techniques, but at each time the giver must be relaxed and calm to enable the flow of chi to occur and thus make the shiatsu work to full effect. As an example, the following exercise on the face and head begins with the receiver's head being held firmly in one hand and, using the thumb of the other hand, pressing upwards in a straight line between the eyebrows towards the hairline. Each movement should only be quite small, about 12 mm (0.5 in). The fingers should then be placed on each side of the head and both thumbs used to press from the inner end of the eyebrows towards the hairline (*see* page 189, A). Again, holding the hands at each side of the head, the thumbs should then be used to press from the start of the eyebrows across the brow to the outside (B). With the fingers in place at each side of the face, work the thumbs across the bone below the eyes, moving approximately 6 mm (0.25 in) at a time (C). Commencing with the thumbs a little to one side of each nostril, press across the face below the cheekbones (*see* page 190, D). Press one thumb in the area between the top lip and nose (E) and then press with both the thumbs outwards over the upper jaw (F). Next, press one thumb in the hollow below the lower lip and then press outwards with both thumbs over the lower part of the jaw (*see* page 191, G). The giver then puts all fingers of the hands beneath the lower jaw and then leans backwards so that pressure is exerted (H).

Kyo and jitsu energy

As a person progresses in the study of shiatsu and comes to understand the needs and requirements of others, he or she will gradually be able to give beneficial therapy. It is believed that energy, as previously defined, is the basis for all life, and it is divided into two types known as *kyo* and *jitsu*. If the energy is low or deficient, it is known as kyo, and if there is an excess or the energy is high, it is known as jitsu. These two factors will therefore affect the type of shiatsu that is given and, with practice, it should be possible to assess visually and also by touch what type a person is. A few general guidelines as to how a person can vary his or her shiatsu to suit either kyo or jitsu types are given below. As the person progresses, however, it is likely that an intuitive awareness will develop of what is most suitable for a particular person. For kyo types (low or deficient

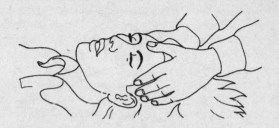

A—press between the eyebrows towards the hairline

B—press from the eyebrows across the brow

C—work the thumbs across the bones below the eyes

D—press across the face below the cheekbones

E—press the area between the nose and upper lip

F—press with thumbs outwards over the upper jaw

G—press outwards over the lower part of the jaw

H—place fingers beneath the jaw and lean back

in energy), a gentle and sensitive touch is required, and any stretched positions can be maintained for a longer time as this will bring more energy to that part of the body. Pressure, held by the thumb or palm, can also be maintained for an increased length of time, approximately 10–15 seconds. For jitsu types (high or excess energy), the stretches can be done quite quickly so that the energy is dispersed, and also shaking or rocking areas of the body can have the same effect. The pressure that is exerted by the thumbs or palms should also be held for a shorter length of time, so that excess energy is dispelled.

Yin and yang

As previously mentioned, a change in diet may also be recommended by a shiatsu practitioner. From the viewpoint of traditional Oriental medicine, food can be defined in an 'energetic' way. This differs from the Western definition of foods consisting of protein, minerals, fats, carbohydrates, fibre and vitamins. It is believed that, according to its 'energetic' definition, food will have differing physical, mental, spiritual and emotional effects. This energy is split into two parts known as *yin* and *yang*. Yin is where energy is expanding and yang where it is contracting. They are thus opposites and, from traditional beliefs, it was thought that interactions between them formed all manner of occurrences in nature and the whole of the world and beyond. All definitions of yin and yang are based on macrobiotic food (a diet intended to prolong life, comprised of pure vegetable foods such as brown rice), this being the most usual reference. Food can be divided into three main types—those that are 'balanced', and some that are yin and some that are yang. Foods that are defined as being yin are milk, alcohol, honey, sugar, oil, fruit juices, spices, stimulants, most drugs (such as aspirin, etc), tropical vegetables and fruits, refined foods, and most food additives of a chemical nature. Yang foods are poultry, seafood, eggs, meat, salt, fish, miso and cheese. Balanced foods are seeds, nuts, vegetables, cereal grains, beans, sea vegetables and temperate fruits (such as apples and pears).

The balance between yin and yang is very important to the body, for example, in the production of hormones such as oestrogen and progesterone, and glycogen and insulin and the expansion and contraction of the lungs, etc. A 'balanced' way of eating, mainly from the grains, beans, seeds, nuts and vegetables, etc, is important as this will help to achieve the energy balance in the meridians, organs and chakras, as defined previ-

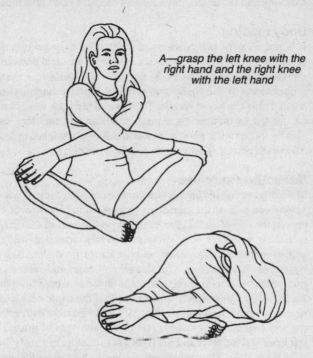

A—grasp the left knee with the right hand and the right knee with the left hand

B—inhale, and as you exhale, lean forwards and downwards with the top half of the body

Makko-ho exercises

ously. When these two opposing forces of yin and yang are in harmony and balanced, physical and mental health will result.

Body reading

It is possible for practitioners of shiatsu, as they become increasingly experienced, to assess a person's physical and mental state of health by observing the body and forming accurate observations. If the traditional ways of Eastern diagnosis are studied, this can assist greatly. The Eastern methods were based on the senses of hearing, seeing, smelling and touching and also by questioning people to obtain information leading to an overall diagnosis. This is known as body reading.

Makko-ho exercises

Makko-ho exercises are six stretching exercises, each of which affects one pair of the meridians by stimulating its flow of energy. If the complete set of exercises is performed, all the body's meridians will have been stimulated in turn, which should result in increased vigour and an absence of tiredness. Before beginning the exercises, you should feel calm and relaxed. It may prove beneficial to perform some abdominal breathing first (as previously described). One example is the triple heater and heart governor meridian stretch. Sit on the ground with either the feet together or crossed. The right hand should grasp the left knee and the left hand the right knee, both quite firmly (*see* A on page 193). Then inhale and, as you exhale, lean forwards and downwards with the top half of the body so that the knees are pushed apart (*see* B on page 192). Hold this position for approximately 30 seconds while breathing normally, and then, after inhaling, return to the upright position. After completion of all exercises, lie flat on the ground for several minutes and relax.

Yoga

Introduction

Origins

From its Indian origins as far back as 4,000 years ago, yoga has been continually practised, but it was only in the 20th century that its use became more widespread. Yoga has an effect on the whole person, combining the physical, mental and spiritual sides. The word 'yoga' is derived from a Sanskrit word that means 'yoke' or 'union' and thus reflects on the practices of yoga being total in effect. For many hundreds of years in India only a select few, such as philosophers and like-minded people with their disciples, followed the way of life that yoga dictated. The leaders were known as 'yogis', and it was they who taught their followers by passing on their accumulated knowledge. These small groups of people dwelt in caves or woods, or sometimes a yogi would live like a hermit. Yoga has had quite far-reaching effects over many hundreds of years in India.

The basics of yoga were defined by a yogi called Patanjali who lived about 300 BC. He was a very well-respected teacher and commanded great influence at that time, and his classification is one that is used now. He established the fact of yoga being separated into eight different parts. The first two concern a person's lifestyle, which should be serene with the days spent in contemplation, study, maintaining cleanliness, and living very simply and at peace with others. Anything that involves avarice or greed, etc, or is harmful to others has to be avoided. The third and fourth parts are concerned with physical matters and list a number of exercises designed to promote peace and infuse energy into both the mind and body. The remaining four sections are concerned with the advancement of a person's soul or spirit and mental faculties by being able to isolate himself or herself from outside worries and normal life, contemplation and broadening mental faculties with the ultimate knowledge known as *somadhi*. Mentally, this is a complete change that gives final realization of existence. Much more recently, yoga became available in India to everyone, in complete contrast to centuries ago. Doctors and teachers taught yoga, and it is now the rule that all schoolchildren have lessons in some of the exercises.

Modern practice

Nowadays, the practice of yoga is not restricted to India alone, with millions of people worldwide being followers. There are actually five different types of yoga: *raja*, *jnana*, *karma* and *bakti*, and *hatha*. It is this last system that is known in the West, and it involves the use of exercises and positions. The other methods concentrate on matters such as control over the mind, appreciation and intelligence or a morally correct way of life. These other methods are regarded as being of equal importance by the person completely committed to yoga as a way of life. Although people may have little or no spiritual feeling, the basic belief of yoga is the importance of mental attitudes in establishing the physical improvements from exercise. Because of media coverage of a famous violinist receiving successful treatment to a damaged shoulder by yoga, it became very popular throughout the United Kingdom. Prior to the 1960s, it was seldom practised, and only then by people who wanted to learn more of Eastern therapies or who had worked and travelled in that area.

It is a belief in yoga that the body's essence of life, or *prana,* analogous to chi, is contained in the breath. Through a change in the way of breathing there can be a beneficial effect on the general health. If a person is in a heightened emotional condition, or similar state, this will have an effect on the breathing. Therefore, if the breathing is controlled or altered this should promote joint feelings of peace and calm, both mentally and emotionally. There is a variety of exercises, and each promotes different types of breathing, such as the rib cage, shoulder and diaphragm. Some of the movements and stances in use were originally devised from the observation of animals, since they appeared to be adept at relaxation and moved with minimum effort. These stances, which are maintained for one or two minutes, aim to increase freedom of movement and make the person aware of the various parts of the body and any stress that may be present. It is not intended that they be physically tiring or that the person should 'show off' in front of others. The aim is to concentrate on self-knowledge.

The treatment

The benefits
It is recommended to follow some simple rules when practising yoga. Firstly, use a fully qualified therapist and practise daily if at all possible. It is advisable to check with a doctor first if a person is undergoing a course of treatment or is on permanent medication, has some sort of infirmity or feels generally unwell. It is always best that yoga is undertaken before meal times, but if this is not possible then three hours must elapse after a large meal or an hour after a light one. Comfortable clothes are essential, and a folded blanket or thick rug should be placed on the ground as the base. Before commenc-

ing yoga, have a bath or shower and repeat this afterwards to gain the maximum benefit. It is not advisable to do yoga if either the bowels or bladder are full. Should the person have been outside on a hot and sunny day it is not recommended that yoga is practised straight afterwards, as feelings of sickness and dizziness may occur.

Yoga is believed to be of benefit to anyone, providing that he or she possesses determination and patience. If a person has certain physical limitations then these must be taken into account with regard to expectations, but there is no age barrier. Teachers believe that people suffering from stress and disorder in their lives are in greater need of a time of harmony and peace. Yoga was used in the main to encourage health in the physical and mental states and thereby act as a preventive therapy. Tension or stress was one of the main disorders for which it was used, but nowadays it has been used for differing disorders such as hypertension (high blood pressure), bronchitis, back pain, headaches, asthma, heart disorders, premenstrual tension and an acid stomach. Trials have also been conducted to assess its potential in treating some illnesses such as multiple sclerosis, cerebral palsy, osteoporosis, rheumatoid arthritis and depression experienced after childbirth. Since the effects of tension are often shown by the tightening and contraction of muscles, the stretching exercises performed in yoga are able to release it. Also, being aware of each muscle as it is stretched encourages a person to lose mentally any stress or problems with which he or she has been beset. Suppleness is developed by the exercises through the use of the bending and twisting actions. This will help to maintain healthy joints, particularly for people who lead rather inactive lives.

There should be no strain felt, and after practice some or all of the exercises can be done in order. As mentioned previously, it is best to check with a qualified therapist if the person is an expectant mother, suffers from hypertension, is overweight or is having her monthly period.

The bow

Lie face down on the ground with the knees bent and then raised in the direction of the head. Then hold the ankles and, while inhaling, a pull should be exerted on the ankles so that the chest, head and thighs are raised up away from the floor. To start with it will not be possible to hold the legs together, but this will gradually occur with regular practice. This position should be maintained for up to ten breaths. To complete the bow, exhale and let go of the legs.

The bow

The bridge

The bridge is carried out on the floor, starting with the person lying on the back, the knees should be bent, with the legs separated a little and the arms at the side of the body. The person should then inhale and lift the torso and legs, thus forming a bridge. The fingers should then be linked under the body and the arms held straight. The person should then incline the body to each side in turn, ensuring that the shoulders stay underneath. To make the bridge a little bigger, pressure can be exerted by the arms and feet. After inhaling, the position should be maintained for a minimum of one minute and the body returned to a relaxed normal position on the floor.

The spinal twist

The spinal twist entails sitting on the floor with the legs outstretched. The left leg should be bent and placed over the other leg as far as possible. The person should exhale and twist the body to the left. The person's right hand should be moved towards the right foot. The person should have the body supported by placing the left hand on the ground at the back but keeping the back straight. Every time the person exhales the body should be further twisted to the left. The position should be maintained for approximately one minute and then the complete action done again, but this time turning to the right. This is a gentle posture that is easy to perform. Relax.

The spinal twist helps to strengthen the spine, improve posture and promote psychological balance.

The triangle

The triangle commences with the person standing upright with the legs apart and the arms held out at shoulder level. Extend the right foot to the side and, upon exhaling, bend over the right-hand side so that the right hand slips downwards in the direction of the ankle. There should be no forward inclination of the body at this time. As the bending action takes place, the left arm should be lifted upright with the palm of the hand to the front. This stretched position should be kept up for the minimum of a minute, with the person trying to extend the stretch as they exhale. After inhaling, the person should then revert to

The bridge

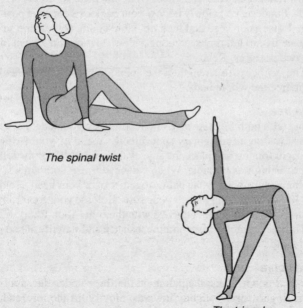

The spinal twist

The triangle

the beginning of the exercise and do it again but leaning in the opposite direction.

The triangle helps to calm the nerves, acts to remove toxins from the body and promotes good health in general.

The cat

Kneel on all fours with your hands shoulder-distance apart and your knees the same distance apart as your hands. Your elbows should remain straight throughout the entire exercise. Exhale while arching your back up high. Keep your head between your arms, looking at your abdomen. Hold this pose for a few seconds. Inhale as you slowly hollow your back to a concave position. Raise your head and look up. Hold again. Repeat the sequence five to ten times, creating a slow flowing movement of the two postures. Relax.

The cat helps to strengthen the spine, improve posture and revitalize the whole body.

The tree

Stand with both feet together, arms loosely by your side. Focus your eyes on an imaginary spot directly ahead of you. Bring the right foot up and place the sole against the inside of the left thigh, as high as possible. When balanced, raise both arms simultaneously, placing the palms together over your head. Hold for 30 seconds. Gently lower your arms. Release your foot from your thigh. Repeat the sequence with the other foot. Relax.

The tree promotes concentration, balance and stability of body and mind.

The cobra

Lie face down. Place the palms on the floor under the shoulders, fingers turned slightly inwards. Slowly lift the forehead, the nose, the chin, and the entire upper body, up to the navel.

The two movements of the cat

The tree

The weight rests on both hands, the pelvis and the legs. Keep the elbows slightly bent, and do not allow the shoulders to hunch up towards the ears. Hold for ten seconds, focusing your attention on the lower back. Very slowly lower your trunk to the floor, then the chin, the nose and the forehead. Relax.

The cobra increases blood supply to the abdominal organs and helps to relieve digestive problems and correct kidney malfunctions.

The plough

Lie on your back, arms by your sides, palms down. Slowly raise your legs and trunk off the floor. Supporting your hips with both hands, bring your legs slightly over your head. Keep your legs as straight as possible. Supporting your back with both hands, continue lifting your legs up and over your head until the toes come to rest on the floor behind your head. Only when you are quite comfortable in the position, release the hold on your back and place your arms flat on the floor. Hold only for ten seconds in the beginning. After your body becomes accustomed to this position, you may hold it longer. Very slowly unroll your body to the starting position. Relax.

The plough helps to reinvigorate the entire nervous system, removing fatigue, listlessness and exhaustion. It is of particular benefit to the pancreas and endocrine glands.

The forward bend

Make sure you are well warmed up before attempting this posture. Sit with your legs stretched out in front of you, knees very straight. Inhale and stretch your arms above your head. Exhale and very slowly and smoothly bend forward from the hips (*not from the waist*) to grasp your toes. If at first this seems difficult,

The cobra

The plough

The forward bend

clasp instead your ankles, calves or knees. It is important that your legs remain straight. Continue to bend forward and down, aiming to touch your knees with your head. Hold for at least ten seconds and observe your breath. Release your hold and very slowly unroll your spine, returning to a sitting position. Repeat twice.

The forward bend slows the respiratory rate to produce a calm and relaxed state of mind. It also increases the suppleness of the spine and improves blood circulation—which helps to regenerate the abdominal organs and improve digestion.

A salute or greeting to the sun

The following twelve stances, known as a greeting to the sun, have the aim of relaxing and invigorating the body and mind. This classic exercise coordinates breathing with variations of six yoga poses in a flowing rhythmic way that stretches and relaxes your body and your mind.

As suggested by its name, it was originally done when the sun rose and when it set. Although these stances are quite safe, they should not be done by pregnant women or those having a monthly period, except with expert tuition. If a person has hypertension (high blood pressure), a hernia, clots in the blood or pain in the lower back they are not recommended. Each exercise should follow on smoothly one after the other.

1 Start by facing east, standing up as straight as you can without forcing it, with your feet together. Inhale and visualize the sun just beginning to rise. Exhale and bring the palms of the hands on to your chest as if you were praying.

2 Then inhale and stretch the arms upright with the palms facing the ceiling and lean backwards, pushing the pelvis forward a little, and look up at your hands.

3 Exhale and, keeping the legs straight, place the fingers or palms on to the ground, ideally your hands are touching the floor in front of or beside your feet. (Don't force this: if you can't reach the floor, let your hands hold on to the lowest part of your legs they can reach.)

4 Whilst inhaling, bend the knees and place one leg straight out backwards, with the knee touching the ground, in a long, lunging movement. Turn your toes right under and straighten your body.

5 With both hands on the ground, raise the head slightly and push the hips to the front. At the same time as holding the breath, stretch the legs out together backwards and raise the body off the floor supported by the arms.

6 Exhale and fold the body over bent knees so that the head touches the ground with the arms stretched out in front, toes curled, until you are in the classic push-up position.

7 After inhaling and exhaling once, drop your knees to the floor, with your bottom up. Bend the elbows and bring your chest and chin to the floor. Continue breathing out and lower the whole body to the floor, straightening your legs and keeping your toes curled under with the body being supported by the hands at shoulder level and also by the toes. The stomach and hips should not be on the ground.

8 After taking a deep breath, stretch the arms and push the body upwards, pushing down on your hands and slowly lifting your head as you straighten the elbows. Arch your back upwards like a snake before it strikes.

9 Exhale and then raise the hips upwards with the feet and hands being kept on the floor so that the body is in an inverted V-shape. The legs and back should be kept straight.

10 Breathe in and lunge forward by bending your right knee and stepping your right foot forward between your hands. When you breathe out, straighten your right leg and bring the left foot next to the right. Lift your buttocks high until you are touching your toes.

11 Inhale and slowly lift the spine, visualizing it unroll one vertebra at a time. Raise your head and look up, bringing your arms straight overhead, and bring the image of the rising sun back to mind.

12 Place the feet together, keeping the legs straight. Breathe out and slowly bring your arms back to the sides, allowing the sun to glow brighter and brighter in your mind's eye.

Salute the sun six times at first, gradually increasing the number of repetitions until you are comfortably doing the routine 24 times. This whole sequence of exercises can be performed several times over if wished. If this is the case, it is suggested to alternate the legs used either forwards or backwards in two of the exercises.

Alternative Therapies

As previously mentioned, yoga has recently been used to treat some illnesses such as rheumatoid arthritis, and if a person has such a severe disorder, then a highly skilled and experienced therapist is essential. Since this form of yoga, known as therapeutic yoga, is so new there is only a limited number of suitably experienced therapists available, although this situation should be remedied by the introduction of further training. For those who wish to use yoga to maintain mental and physical health, joining a class with an instructor is perhaps the best way to proceed, so that exercises are performed correctly and any lapses in concentration can be corrected. These classes last usually in the region of an hour and are separated into sessions for beginners and those who are more proficient. Proficiency and progress are achieved by frequent practice, which can be done at home between lessons. One simple exercise that helps reduce stress is quite simple to perform and does not take long. The person should lie on the floor with the arms at the side and the legs together. After inhaling, all the muscles from the toes to the thighs should be tightened in turn. As the person exhales, the muscles in the stomach up to the shoulders should then be tightened, including the hands, which should be clenched. After inhaling again, the chest, throat and face muscles should be tightened, as well as screwing up the face, and this should be maintained until the next breath has to be taken. All muscles should then be relaxed, the legs parted and the arms spread out comfortably with the palms facing the ceiling. The person should then totally relax with a sensation of falling through the ground.

The majority of doctors regard yoga as a type of exercise that is beneficial, although some do recommend patients to refer to yoga practitioners. However, if a specific disorder is to be treated, it is very important that the ailment should first be seen by a doctor.

Aromatherapy

Healing through aromatherapy

Aromatherapy is a method of healing using very concentrated essential oils that are often highly aromatic and are extracted from plants. Constituents of the oils confer the characteristic perfume or odour given off by a particular plant. Essential oils help the plant in some way to complete its cycle of growth and reproduction. For example, some oils may attract insects for the purpose of pollination; others may render it distasteful as a source of food. Any part of a plant—the stems, leaves, flowers, fruits, seeds, roots or bark—may produce essential oils or essences but often only in minute amounts. Different parts of the same plant may produce their own form of oil. An example of this is the orange, which produces oils with different properties in the flowers, fruits and leaves.

Art and writings from the ancient civilizations of Egypt, China and Persia show that plant essences were used and valued by priests, physicians and healers. Plant essences have been used throughout the ages for healing—in incense for religious rituals, in perfumes and embalming ointments and for culinary purposes. There are many Biblical references that give an insight into the uses of plant oils and the high value that was attached to them. Throughout the course of human history the healing properties of plants and their essential oils have been recognized and most people probably had some knowledge about their use. It was only in more recent times, with the great developments in science and orthodox medicine, particularly the manufacture of antibiotics and synthetic drugs, that knowledge and interest in the older methods of healing declined. However, in the last few years there has been a great rekindling of interest in the practice of aromatherapy with many people turning to this form of treatment.

Techniques used in aromatherapy

Massage

Massage is the most familiar method of treatment associated with aromatherapy. Essential oils are able to penetrate through the skin and are taken into the body, exerting healing and beneficial influences on internal tissues and organs. The oils used for massage are first diluted by being mixed with a base and should never be applied directly to the skin in their pure form in case of an adverse allergic reaction.

An aromatherapist will 'design' an individual whole-body massage based on an accurate history taken from the patient and much experience in the use of essential oils. The oils will be chosen specifically to match the temperament of the patient and also to deal with any particular medical or emotional problems which may be troubling him or her.

Although there is no substitute for a long soothing aromatherapy massage given by an expert, the techniques are not difficult to learn and can be carried out satisfactorily at home.

Bathing

Bathing most people have experienced the benefits of relaxing in a hot bath to which a proprietary perfumed preparation has been added. Most of these preparations contain essential oils used in aromatherapy. The addition of a number of drops of an essential oil to the bath water is soothing and relaxing, easing aches and pains, and can also have a stimulating effect, banishing tiredness and restoring energy. In addition, there is the added benefit of inhaling the vapours of the oil as they evaporate from the hot water.

Inhalation

Inhalation is thought to be the most direct and rapid means of treatment. This is because the molecules of the volatile essential oil act directly on the olfactory organs and are immediately perceived by the brain. A popular method is the time-honoured one of steam inhalation, in which a few drops of essential oil are added to hot water in a bowl. The person sits with his or her face above the mixture and covers the head, face and bowl with a towel so that the vapours do not escape and are inhaled. This can be repeated up to three times a day but should not be undertaken by people suffering from asthma. Some essential oils can be applied directly to a handkerchief or onto a pillow and the vapours inhaled in this way.

Steam inhalation with essential oils constitutes a wonderful, time-honoured way of alleviating the symptoms of colds and flu, and can also be beneficial to greasy skins. Steam inhalations should, however, be avoided by asthmatics unless under direction from a medical practitioner, as the steam can occasionally irritate the lungs.

Compresses

Compresses are effective in the treatment of a variety of muscular and rheumatic aches and pains as well as bruises and headaches. To prepare a compress, add five drops of oil to a small bowl of water. Soak a piece of flannel or other absorbent material in the solution. Squeeze out excess moisture (although the compress should remain fairly wet) and secure in position with a bandage or clingfilm. For acute pain, the compress should be renewed when it has reached blood temperature, otherwise it should be left in position for a minimum of two hours and preferably overnight. Cold water should be used wherever fever or acute pain or hot swelling require treatment, whereas the water should be hot if the pain is chronic. If fever is present, the compress should be changed frequently.

Hair treatments/scalp tonics

Many hair conditions, such as dryness, excessive grease or dandruff, will respond to aromatherapy using specific recipes of essential oils diluted in a nourishing base oil. For instance, 60 drops of an essential oil diluted in 100 mls (3.5 fl oz) of base oil (such as olive or sweet almond) will make a wonderful conditioning treatment. Simply rub the oils thoroughly into the scalp, then wrap the hair in warm towels and allow the oil to penetrate the hair and the scalp for an hour or two. The choice of oil depends, of course, upon the desired effect: chamomile and rosemary, for instance, will condition and promote healthy hair growth, bergamot and tea tree are helpful in dandruff control whilst lavender has repellent qualities that will deter lice and fleas.

Face creams, oils and lotions

For the face, essential oils should be mixed with base oils in much the same way as for massage, the main difference being that more nourishing oils such as apricot kernel and avocado should be used in preference to ordinary vegetable oils. (It should be noted that avocado is a fairly heavy oil and its use is best reserved for dry skin.) Essential oils can also be added to a non-perfumed cold cream or lotion and used for problem complexions.

Most essential oils have antiseptic properties and can be used to treat infective skin conditions. Certain oils (such as rose and neroli) are anti-inflammatory and have a soothing effect, whereas sandalwood is useful in the treatment of superficial broken veins. Rose and neroli are also excellent for care of mature skins. For dry cracked skin, the addition of wheatgerm and avocado oil (with their high vitamin E content) to preparations will relieve the condition. In general, aromatherapy can improve the skin by encouraging toxin removal, stimulating cell growth and renewal, and improving circulation. A gentle circular massage with the tips of the fingers should be used on the face, and special care must be taken not to stretch or drag the delicate skin around the eye area.

Flower waters

Flower waters constitute a refreshing and soothing aid in the treatment and prevention of skin conditions such as eczema and acne, and can be easily prepared at home. Simply add around 20 drops of essential oil to an amber glass bottle containing 100 mls (3.5 fl oz) of spring water, then leave it to stand in a dark place for a few days. Filter the water through some coffee or similar filter paper, then apply to the skin as required, using a cotton wool pad.

Bathing and showering

Add a few drops (5–10) of essential oil to the bath water after the water has been drawn, then close the door to retain the aromatic vapours. The choice of oils is entirely up to the individual, depending on the desired effect, although those with sensitive skins are advised to have the oils ready diluted in a base oil prior to bathing.

Bathing in essential oils can stimulate and revive or relax and sedate, depending on the oils selected: rosemary and pine can have a soothing effect on tired or aching limbs, chamomile and lavender are popular for relieving insomnia and anxiety, etc. A similar effect (although obviously not quite as relaxing) can be achieved whilst showering by soaking a wet sponge in an essential oil mix, then rubbing it over the body under the warm spray.

Sitz bath

A sitz, or shallow, bath in the appropriate essential oil can bring enormous relief in conditions such as haemorrhoids, thrush and cystitis (*see also* page 43).

Foot bath

Tired, swollen feet can be refreshed by bathing in a basin of hot water containing 4–5 drops of lavender, peppermint, rosemary or thyme.

Hands

Dry, chapped hands may be soothed by soaking in a bowl of warm water containing a few drops of essential oil such as patchouli or rose.

Mouthwash and gargles

Used strictly in the correct dilutions, essential oils provide a natural, gentle way to help clear up mouth ulcers, oral thrush and infected gums, but it cannot be stressed too much that essential oils should never be swallowed.

Neat application and internal use

Generally, the application of undiluted essential oils directly to the skin should be avoided as many are highly irritant. However, there are one or two exceptions that have been safely applied to the skin undiluted for centuries. These include lemon oil, which can be applied neat to warts (Vaseline can be applied around the wart to protect the surrounding skin); lavender, which can be safely applied directly to burns, cuts, bites and stings; and tea tree, which may be dabbed on spots. Any other oils must be used in dilution unless under careful direction from a trained aromatherapist.

Many essential oils are highly toxic when taken orally and there are *no circumstances* in which they may safely be taken at home in this way.

Mode of action of essential oils

Although the subject of a great deal of research, there is a lack of knowledge about how essential oils work in the body to produce their therapeutic effects. It is known that individual essential oils possess antiseptic, antibiotic, sedative, tonic and stimulating properties, and it is believed that they act in harmony with the natural defences of the body such as the immune system. Some oils, such as eucalyptus and rosemary, act as natural decongestants whereas others, such as sage, have a beneficial effect upon the circulation.

Conditions that may benefit from aromatherapy

A wide range of conditions and disorders may benefit from aromatherapy, and it is considered to be a gentle treatment suitable for all age groups. It is especially beneficial for long-term chronic conditions, and the use of essential oils is believed by therapists to prevent the development of some illnesses. Conditions that may be relieved by aromatherapy include painful limbs, muscles and joints resulting from arthritic or rheumatic disorders, respiratory complaints, digestive disorders, skin conditions, throat and mouth infections, urinary tract infections and problems affecting the hair and scalp. Also, period pains, burns, insect bites and stings, headaches, high blood pressure, feverishness, menopausal symptoms, poor circulation and gout can benefit from aromatherapy. Aromatherapy is also of great benefit in relieving stress and stress-related symptoms such as anxiety, insomnia and depression.

Many of the essential oils can be safely used at home and the basic techniques of use can soon be mastered. However, some should only be used by a trained aromatherapist and others must be avoided in certain conditions such as pregnancy. In some circumstances, massage is not considered to be advisable. It is wise to seek medical advice in the event of doubt or if the ailment is more than a minor one.

Consulting a professional aromatherapist

Aromatherapy is a holistic approach to healing, hence the practitioner endeavours to build up a complete picture of the patient and his or her lifestyle, nature and family circumstances, as well as noting the symptoms that need to be to be treated. Depending upon the picture that is obtained, the aromatherapist decides upon the essential oil or oils that are most suitable and likely to prove most helpful in the circumstances that prevail. The aromatherapist has a wide-ranging knowledge and experience upon which to draw. Many oils can be blended together for an enhanced effect, and this is called a 'synergistic blend'. Many aromatherapists offer a massage and/or instruction on the use of the selected oils at home.

Base oils

Because essential oils are extremely concentrated and also because of their tendency to evaporate rapidly, they need to be diluted with carrier or base oils. Generally it is not advised that essential oils should be applied undiluted to the skin, although there are one or two specific exceptions. It is very important to use a high quality base oil, as oils such as baby oil or mineral oil have very poor penetrating qualities, which will hamper the passage of the essential oil through the skin. Indeed, it would be better to use a good quality vegetable or nut oil for babies in preference to proprietary baby oils as the vegetable oil is more easily absorbed and contains more nutrients.

Although the choice of base oil is largely a matter of personal preference, it is useful to note that many vegetable oils possess therapeutic properties of their own. Sweet almond, soya bean, sunflower, jojoba, olive, grapeseed, hazelnut, avocado, corn or safflower oil will all provide a suitable base for essential oils, although these should preferably be of the cold-pressed variety which has higher nutrient levels.

Pure essential oils should retain their potency for one to two years, but once diluted in a base oil will last for only three months or so before spoiling. They should also be stored at a fairly constant room temperature in corked dark glass bottles or flip-top containers as they will deteriorate quickly when subjected to extremes of light and temperature. Adding some vitamin E or wheatgerm oil to the mixture can help prolong its usefulness. For massage oils, it is best to make up a very small quantity of essential oil in base oil for each application because of its poor keeping qualities.

Below is a very rough guide to the dilution of essential oils. However, you will find many variations and differing opinions on this depending on the preference of individual therapists, and their recipes will differ accordingly.

Base Oil	Essential Oil
100 ml (3.5 fl oz)	20-60 drops
25 ml	7-25 drops
1 teaspoon (5 ml)	3-5 drops

Blending essential oils

Essences can be blended to treat specific ailments, and some aromatherapy books contain precise recipes for blends. When two or more essential oils are working together in harmony, this is known as a synergistic blend. Obviously, it takes many years of experience to know which combinations of plant essences will work most effectively together, but as a rough guide, oils extracted from plants of the same botanical family will usually blend and work well together, although it is by no means necessary to stick rigidly to this rule as other combinations may be just as successful. Really, a number of factors need to be taken into account when preparing a blend of oils for a patient, such as the nature of his or her complaint, personality or frame of mind. For home use, it is not usually beneficial to blend more than three oils for any one preparation.

Around the home

There are a variety of ways in which your home can be enhanced by the use of essential oils. Fragrances, pomanders, ring burners and diffusers can all be used in conjunction with essential oils to impart a wonderful scent to a room. (Essential oils should be put into water and vapourized and not burned as they are inflammable. Follow the instructions on ring burners carefully and never put essential oils directly onto a hot light bulb.) Most essential oils also have antimicrobial properties, which make them extremely useful when the occupants of the room are suffering from colds and flu. Oils such as myrtle and eucalyptus also seem to have a soothing effect on coughs and can be used in the bedroom where they will release their aroma throughout the night.

Fragrancers, pomanders and ring burners can all be purchased quite cheaply from shops, and indeed make very welcome gifts, but it is not neccessary to use any extra equipment to benefit from essential oils in the home. By adding a few drops of essential oil to a bowl of warm water or soaking a cotton ball in the oil and placing it in a warm place the same effect can be achieved. You can also sprinkle logs and twigs before placing them on the fire or barbecue to create a soothing aroma.

In case of colds or flu, a bowl of water is actually preferable as it has a humidifying effect on the air. Three or four drops of an appropriate essential oil such as eucalyptus or cypress sprinkled on a handkerchief can also be inhaled periodically to alleviate the worst symptoms of sinusitis, colds and headaches. Similarly, 2–3 drops of a relaxing essential oil on the pillow at night can help to alleviate insomnia.

How essential oils work

Inhalation, application and bathing are the three main methods used to encourage the entry of essential oils into the body. When inhaled, the extremely volatile oils may enter via the olfactory system, and permeation of the skin occurs when they are diluted and applied externally. By bathing in essential oils, we can inhale and absorb the oils through the skin simultaneously.

Little is known about how essential oils actually affect the mind and the body, although research is currently ongoing in the United States of America and the United Kingdom. However, the effectiveness of aromatherapy has been supported by recent research in central Europe, the United States of America, the United Kingdom and Australia. It appears that most essential oils are antiseptic and bactericidal to some degree, whilst some even seem to be effective in fighting viral infections.

On inhalation, essential oil molecules are received by receptor cells in the lining of the nose, which will transmit signals to the brain. Electrochemical messages received by the olfactory centre in the brain then stimulate the release of powerful neurochemicals into the blood which will then be transported around the body. Molecules inhaled into the lungs may pass into the bloodstream and be disseminated in the same way.

When rubbed or massaged into the skin, essential oils will permeate the pores and hair follicles. From here, they can readily pass into the tiny blood vessels (known as capillaries), by virtue of their molecular structure, and then travel around the body.

Following absorption, the action of the oil depends upon its chemical constituents. Most essential oils are high in alcohols and esters, although a few contain a high concentration of phenols, aldehydes and ketones. The latter are powerful chemicals so the use of oils containing them should be avoided by all save the skilled professional.

Special care
You may find that your professional aromatherapist will use some of the following oils, but these are generally unsafe for use by the lay person.

Generally
Aniseed, cinamon bark, cinamon leaf, clove bud, clove leaf, clove stem, fennel (bitter), pine, parsley, nutmeg.

During pregnancy
Basil, cedarwood, clary sage, fennel, juniper, marjoram, myrrh, rosemary, sage, thyme, parsley, nutmeg.

Prior to exposure to sun
Bergamot, lemon, mandarin, orange, fennel.

Hypertension
Sage, thyme, cypress.

Aromatherapy massage at home

Before beginning an aromatherapy massage, there are a number of steps that should be taken in order for the subject of the massage to derive full benefit from the treatment:

(1) It is important to take a brief history from the patient in order to be able to select the correct oils. This will involve an assessment of his or her emotional state as well as any physical complaints.

(2) At least an hour should have elapsed since the last meal prior to receiving or giving a massage.

(3) Make sure your clothing is loose and will not obstruct your movements.

(4) Ensure that hands are clean and nails short.

(5) Have some tissues ready, and make sure your oil is easily accessible.

(6) Make sure your hands are warm before touching your subject.

The room should be warm so that your subject will be comfortable even though only partly dressed. Lighting should be subdued, and the telephone should be disconnected to avoid interruption. Perhaps music could be played softly in the background, but this is a matter of preference and convenience. It is a good idea to have a compatible essence evaporating in the room prior to commencement. The massage surface needs to be firm, therefore a normal sprung bed is unsuitable—instead, pad the floor or use a futon or similar firm mattress.

First of all the subject may have a warm bath or shower in order that the pores are open and receptive to the essential oil.

This, however, is a matter of personal preference on the part of the therapist. The subject should be positioned comfortably and should be covered with towels, exposing only the area that is to be massaged at any one time in order to avoid embarrassment and cold. Hair should be tied out of the way.

Basic techniques

The following constitutes only a very basic guide to massage movements and is no substitute for a comprehensive aromamassage course. However, massage can be used to great benefit at home using the following simple movements and suggestions:

Effleurage

This is the most often used therapy movement, and constitutes a simple, gentle stroking movement (*see* diagrams on page 62). Note that deep pressure should *never* be used by an untrained person. The strokes may be long or short, gentle or firm, but the whole hand should be used, always pushing the blood towards the heart, thus promoting venous return. This stroke promotes muscle relaxation and soothes the nerve endings.

Petrissage

In petrissage, the flesh is gently rolled between the thumbs and fingers in a movement not unlike kneading dough (*see* diagrams on page 63). This technique is best used on the back and on fatty areas. The idea is to stimulate the circulation and lymphatic flow and thereby increase the rate of toxin expulsion.

Neck and shoulder massage

Neck massage should be carried out with the patient sitting on a chair with some support in front. Working around the base of the neck and scalp, use small upward and outward circular movements. Move slowly up, down and around the sides of the neck, alternating firm and gentle movements.

Using gentle anticlockwise effleurage movements, stroke firmly from the shoulders to the neck (*see* diagrams on page 65).

Back massage
Avoiding the vertebrae, use gentle or firm petrissage or effleurage movements. Stroke all the way from the lumbar to the shoulders, move the hands outwards across the shoulders and return slowly down the outer area of the back. Repeat this movement to induce deep relaxation (*see* diagrams on pages 67–68).

Limb massage
For leg massage, always massage the legs in an upward direction (*see* diagrams on page 69). Avoid bony areas and *never* massage varicose veins.

For feet massage, work in the direction of toe to heel, using the fingers uppermost and the thumb under the foot (*see* diagrams on page 69).

For arm massage, use effleurage and petrissage movements upwards in the direction of the armpit, concentrating on muscular and fatty areas. Avoid bony areas (*see* diagrams on page 71).

Head massage
Put a little of the essential massage oil on the fingertips and massage in circular movements over the scalp and temples (*see* diagrams on page 73).

Massage for tension headaches and migraine
Work from the base of the neck and scalp for a few moments, using effleurage strokes firmly, again with the chosen oil(s) on the fingertips.

Abdomenal massage

Use a clockwise effleurage stroke, taking care not to apply too much pressure.

Massage for menstrual or gynaecological problems

Always use gentle effleurage movements and do not exert any pressure on the lower abdomen. Begin at the lower back and slide forwards and downwards across the hips. Repeat several times.

Common ailments

Below are listed some disorders that can be alleviated by the use of essential oils. Special care should be taken when using the oils marked with an asterisk (*). When employed incorrectly they can have adverse effects and are normally recommended to be used only under the guidance of a professional aromatherapist. See also the section on Special care, page 222.

Stress-related disorders

Anxiety   basil, bergamot, geranium, lavender, marjoram (sweet), melissa, neroli, sandalwood, vetiver.

Mild shock   basil, chamomile, melissa, peppermint, rosemary.

Depression   bergamot, chamomile, geranium, jasmine, lavender, neroli, patchouli, rose, rosemary, sage*.

Fatigue   clary sage, eucalyptus, juniper berry, peppermint, rosemary.

Skin complaints/disorders

Dry skin   bergamot, chamomile, geranium, jasmine,

	lavendar, melissa, neroli, patchouli, sandalwood, ylang ylang.
Oily skin	cypress, lemon, tea tree.
Acne	bergamot, cedarwood, chamomile, cypress, eucalyptus, fennel, geranium, juniper berry, lavender, lemon, myrrh, parsley*, patchouli, petitgrain, rose, rosemary, sandalwood, tea tree.
Eczema	chamomile, geranium, juniper berry, lavender, melissa.
Psoriasis	bergamot, chamomile, eucalyptus, lavender, peppermint.

Feminine/gynaeological disorders

Amenorrhoea	chamomile, clary sage, fennel, geranium, sage*.
Dysmenorrhoea	cypress, geranium, rose.
Hot flushes	chamomile, clary sage, jasmine, lavender, neroli, petitgrain, sandalwood, ylang ylang.
Mastitis	chamomile, clary sage, geranium, lavender, rose.
Period pain	clary sage, lavender, marjoram
PMT	geranium, lavender, neroli, petitgrain, rose.

Herbal Remedies

History of the use of herbal remedies

Herbalism is sometimes maligned as a collection of home-made remedies to be applied in a placebo fashion to one symptom or another, provided the ailment is not too serious and provided there is a powerful chemical wonder-drug at the ready to suppress any 'real' symptoms. We often forget, however, that botanical medicine provides a complete system of healing and disease prevention. It is the oldest and most natural form of medicine. Its record of efficacy and safety spans centuries and covers every country worldwide. Because herbal medicine is holistic medicine, it is, in fact, able to look beyond the symptoms to the underlying systemic imbalance; when skilfully applied by a trained practitioner, herbal medicine offers very real and permanent solutions to concrete problems, many of them seemingly intractable to pharmaceutical intervention.

Early civilizations

The medicinal use of herbs is said to be as old as mankind itself. In early civilizations, food and medicine were linked and many plants were eaten for their health-giving properties. In ancient Egypt, the slave workers were given a daily ration of garlic to help fight off the many fevers and infections that were common at that time. The first written records of herbs and their beneficial properties were compiled by the ancient Egyptians. Most of our knowledge and use of herbs can be traced back to the Egyptian priests who also practised herbal medicine. Records dating back to 1500 BC listed medicinal herbs, including caraway and cinnamon.

The ancient Greeks and Romans also carried out herbal medicine, and as they invaded new lands their doctors encountered new herbs and introduced herbs such as rosemary or lavender into new areas. Other cultures with a history of herbal medicine are the Chinese and the Indians. In Britain, the use of herbs developed along with the establishment of monasteries around the country, each of which had its own herb garden for use in treating both the monks and the local people. In some areas, particularly Wales and Scotland, Druids and other Celtic healers are thought to have had an oral tradition of herbalism, where medicine was mixed with religion and ritual.

The first publications

Over time, these healers and their knowledge led to the writing of the first 'herbals', which rapidly rose in importance and distribution upon the advent of the printing press in the 15th century. John Parkinson of London wrote a herbal around 1630, listing useful plants. Many herbalists set up their own apothecary shops, including the famous Nicholas Culpepper (1616–54) whose most famous work is *The Complete Herbal and English Physician, Enlarged*, published in 1649. Then, in 1812, Henry Potter started a business supplying herbs and dealing in leeches. By this time a huge amount of traditional knowledge and folklore on medicinal herbs was available from Britain, Europe, the Middle East, Asia and the Americas. This promoted Potter to write *Potter's Encyclopaedia of Botanical Drugs and Preparations*, which is still published today.

The decline of herbal medicine

It was in this period, the 19th century, that scientifically inspired conventional medicine rose in popularity, sending herbal medicine into a decline. In rural areas, herbal medicine continued to thrive in local folklore, traditions and practices. In 1864 the National Association (later Institute) of Medical Herbalists was established to organize training of herbal medicine practitioners and to maintain standards of practice. From 1864 until the early part of the 20th century the Institute fought attempts to ban herbal medicine, and over time public interest in herbal medicine increased. This move away from synthetic drugs results partly from to possible side effects, bad publicity and, in some instances, a mistrust of the medical and pharmacological industries. The more natural appearance of herbal remedies has led to its growing support and popularity. Herbs from America have been incorporated with common remedies, and scientific research into herbs and their active ingredients has confirmed their healing power and enlarged the range of medicinal herbs used today.

Its rise and relevance today

Herbal medicine can be viewed as the precursor of modern pharmacology, but today it continues as an effective and more natural method of treating and preventing illness. Globally, herbal medicine is three to four times more commonly practised than conventional medicine.

Nowhere is the efficacy of herbalism more evident than in problems related to the nervous system. Stress, anxiety, tension and depression are intimately connected with most illness. Few health practitioners would argue with the influence of nervous anxiety in pathology. Nervous tension is generally acknowledged by doctors to contribute to duodenal and gastric ulceration, ulcerative colitis, irritable bowel syndrome and many other gut-related disorders.

We know also, from physiology, that when a person is depressed, the secretion of hydrochloric acid—one of the main digestive juices—is also reduced so that digestion and absorption are rendered less efficient. Anxiety, on the other hand, can lead to the release of adrenaline and stimulate the overproduction of hydrochloric acid and result in a state of acidity that may exacerbate the pain of an inflamed ulcer. In fact, whenever the voluntary nervous system (our conscious anxiety) interferes with the autonomic processes (the automatic nervous regulation that in health is never made conscious), illness is the result.

Herbalists rely on their knowledge of botanical remedies to rectify this type of human malfunction. The medical herbalist will treat a stubborn dermatological problem by using 'alternatives' specific to the skin problem and then applying circulatory stimulants to aid in the removal of toxins from the area, with remedies to reinforce other organs of elimination, such as the liver and kidneys. Under such natural treatment, free of any discomforting side effects, the patient can feel confident and relaxed—perhaps for the first time in many months.

Curiously, this is an approach that has never been taken up by orthodox medicine. There, the usual treatment of skin problems involves suppression of symptoms with steroids. However, the use of conventional antihistamines or benzodiazepines often achieves less lasting benefit to the patient because of the additional burden of side effects, such as drowsiness, increased toxicity and long-term drug dependence.

Herbs, on the other hand, are free from toxicity and habituation. Because they are organic substances and not synthetic molecules, they possess an affinity with the human organism. They are extremely efficient in balancing the nervous system. Restoring a sense of wellbeing and relaxation is necessary for optimum health and for the process of self-healing.

Naturally, the choice of a treatment should be based upon a thorough health assessment and the experience and training of a qualified herbal practitioner. The herbalist will then prepare and prescribe herbal remedies in a variety of different forms, such as infusions, loose teas, suppositories, inhalants, lotions, tinctures, tablets and pills. Many of these preparations are available for home use from chemists, health shops and mail-order suppliers.

Herbs for stress management

Chamomile
This has a relaxing effect on the mind and body. It is an excellent sedative for anxiety and muscle tenseness. Many people enjoy its benefits in the form of chamomile tea.

Valerian
This is the ideal tranquillizer. The rhizomes of this plant contain a volatile oil (which includes valerianic acid), volatile alkaloids and iridoids, which have been shown to reduce anxiety and aggression. So effective is valerian in relieving anxiety while maintaining normal mental awareness that it enables us to continue the most complicated mental exercise without drowsiness, loss of consciousness or depression. Valerian has been usefully taken before an examination or a driving test!

Peppermint
This is effective for treating digestive discomfort: it relieves indigestion, flatulence, constipation and nausea. Peppermint is also a good mind tonic, helping to clarify ideas and focus concentration. It is also helpful in alleviating the symptoms of colds and flu. Peppermint and chamomile tea is thought to be effective in reducing the pain of tension headaches and migraines.

St John's wort

Also called *Hypericum perforatum*, St John's wort has analgesic and anti-inflammatory properties, with important local applications to neuralgia and sciatica. Its sedative properties are based on the glycoside hypericin (a red pigment), which makes it applicable to neurosis and irritability. Many herbalists use it extensively as a background remedy.

Lemon balm

This herb relieves flatulance and spasms and is active specifically on that part of the vagus nerve that may interfere with the harmonious functioning of the heart and the stomach. Recent research has indicated that the action of the volatile oil begins within the system of the brain concerned with basic emotions and subsequently operates directly upon the vagus nerve and all the organs that are affected by it. Accordingly, neurasthenia (complete nervous prostration), migraine and nervous disorders of the stomach are amenable to its healing power.

Lime flowers

These are thought to be helpful in controlling anxiety and hyperactivity. They are also effective for treating insomnia, high blood pressure and for soothing muscles and nerves.

Borage

This is an effective mind tonic, which helps to alleviate headaches, migraine and depression.

Oats

Oats are one of the great herbal restoratives of the nervous system. The plant contains an alkaloid that is helpful in angina and in cardiac insufficiency. It has also been used in the treatment of addiction to morphine, narcotics, tobacco and alcohol.

Homeopathy

Introduction

The aim of homeopathy is to cure an illness or disorder by treating the whole person rather than merely concentrating on a set of symptoms. Hence, in homeopathy the approach is holistic, and the overall state of health of the patient, especially his or her emotional and psychological wellbeing, is regarded as being significant. A homeopath notes the symptoms that the person wishes to have cured but also takes time to discover other signs or indications of disorder that the patient may regard as being less important. The reasoning behind this is that illness is a sign of disorder or imbalance within the body. It is believed that the whole 'make-up' of a person determines, to a great extent, the type of disorders to which that individual is prone and the symptoms likely to occur. A homeopathic remedy must be suitable both for the symptoms and the characteristics and temperament of the patient. Hence, two patients with the same illness may be offered different remedies according to their individual natures. One remedy may also be used to treat different groups of symptoms or ailments.

Like cures like

Homeopathic remedies are based on the concept that 'like cures like', an ancient philosophy that can be traced back to the 5th century BC, when it was formulated by Hippocrates. In the early 1800s, this idea awakened the interest of a German doctor, Samuel Hahnemann, who believed that the medical practices at the time were too harsh and tended to hinder rather than aid healing. Hahnemann observed that a treatment for malaria, based on an extract of cinchona bark (quinine), actually produced symptoms of this disease when taken in a small dose by a healthy person. Further extensive studies convinced him that the production of symptoms was the body's way of combating illness. Hence, to give a minute dose of a substance that stimulated the symptoms of an illness in a healthy person could be used to fight that illness in someone who was sick. Hahnemann conducted numerous trials (called 'provings'), giving minute doses of substances to healthy people and recording the symptoms produced. Eventually, these very dilute remedies were given to people with illnesses, often with encouraging results.

Modern homeopathy is based on the work of Hahnemann, and the medicines derived from plant, mineral and animal sources are used in extremely dilute amounts. Indeed, it is believed that the curative properties are enhanced by each dilution because impurities that might cause unwanted side effects are lost. Substances used in homeopathy are first soaked in alcohol to extract their essential ingredients. This initial solution, called the 'mother tincture', is diluted successively either by factors of ten (called the 'decimal scale' and designated X) or 100 (the 'centesimal scale' and designated C). Each dilution is shaken vigorously before further ones are made, and this is thought to make the properties more powerful by adding energy at each stage while impurities are removed. The thorough shakings of each dilution are said to energize, or 'potentiate', the medicine. The remedies are made into tablets or may be used in the form of ointment, solutions, powders, suppositories, etc. High potency (i.e. more dilute) remedies are used for severe symptoms and lower potency (less dilute) for milder ones.

The homeopathic view is that during the process of healing, symptoms are redirected from more important to less important body systems. It is also held that healing is from innermost to outermost parts of the body and that more recent symptoms disappear first, this being known as the 'law of direction of cure'. Occasionally, symptoms may worsen initially when a homeopathic remedy is taken, but this is usually short-lived and is known as a 'healing crisis'. It is taken to indicate a change and that improvement is likely to follow. Usually, with a homeopathic remedy, an improvement is noticed fairly quickly although this depends upon the nature of the ailment, health, age and wellbeing of the patient and potency of the remedy.

A first homeopathic consultation is likely to last about one hour so that the specialist can obtain a full picture of the patient's medical history and personal circumstances. On the basis of this information, the homeopathic doctor decides on an appropriate remedy and potency (which is usually 6C). Subsequent consultations are generally shorter, and full advice is given on how to store and take the medicine. It is widely accepted that homeopathic remedies are safe and non-addictive, but they are covered by the legal requirements governing all medicines and should be obtained from a recognized source.

The development of homeopathy

The Greek physician Hippocrates, who lived several hundred years before the birth of Christ (460–370 BC), is regarded as the founding father of all medicine. The Hippocratic Oath taken by newly qualified doctors in orthodox medicine binds them to an ethical code of medical practice in honour of Hippocrates. Hippocrates believed that disease resulted from natural elements in the world in which people lived. This contrasted with the view that held sway for centuries that disease was some form of punishment from the gods or God. He believed that it was essential to observe and take account of the course and progress of a disease in each individual, and that any cure should encourage that person's own innate healing power. Hippocrates embraced the idea of 'like being able to cure like' and had many remedies that were based on this principle. Hence, in his practice and study of medicine he laid the foundations of the homeopathic approach although this was not to be appreciated and developed for many centuries.

During the period of Roman civilization a greater knowledge and insight into the nature of the human body was developed. Many herbs and plants were used for healing by people throughout the world, and much knowledge was gained and handed down from generation to generation. The belief persisted, however, that diseases were caused by supernatural or divine forces. It was not until the early 1500s that a Swiss doctor, Paracelsus (1493–1541), put forward the view that disease resulted from external environmental forces. He also believed that plants and natural substances held the key to healing and embraced the 'like can cure like' principle. One of his ideas, known as the 'doctrine of signatures', was that the appearance of a plant, or the substances it contained, gave an idea of the disorders it could cure.

In the succeeding centuries, increased knowledge was gained about the healing properties of plants and the way the human body worked. In spite of this, the methods of medical practice were extremely harsh, and there is no doubt that many people suffered needlessly and died because of the treatment they received. It was against this background that Samuel Hahnemann (1755–1843), the founding father of modern homeopathy, began his work as a doctor in the late 1700s. In his early writings, Hahnemann criticized the severe practices of medicine and advocated a healthy diet, clean living conditions and high standards of hygiene as a means of improving health and warding off disease. In 1790, he became interested in quinine, extracted from the bark of the cinchona tree, which was known to be an effective treatment for malaria. He tested the substance first on himself, and later on friends and close family members, and recorded the results. These 'provings' led him to conduct many further investigations and provings of other natural substances, during the course of which he rediscovered and established the principle of like being able to cure like.

By 1812, the principle and practice of homeopathy had become established, and many other doctors adopted the homeopathic approach. Hahnemann himself became a teacher in homeopathy at the University of Leipzig and published many important writings—the results of his years of research. He continued to practise, teach and conduct research throughout his life, especially in producing more dilute remedies that were succussed, or shaken, at each stage and were found to be more potent. Although his work was not without its detractors, Hahnemann had attracted a considerable following by the 1830s. In 1831 there was a widespread cholera epidemic in central Europe for which Hahnemann recommended treatment with camphor. Many people were cured, including Dr Frederick Quin (1799–1878), a medical practitioner at that time. He went on to establish the first homeopathic hospital in London in 1849. A later resurgence of cholera in Britain enabled the effectiveness of camphor to be established beyond doubt, as the numbers of people cured at the homeopathic hospital were far greater than those treated at other hospitals.

In the United States of America, homeopathy became firmly established in the early part of the 19th century, and there were several eminent practitioners who further enhanced knowledge and practice. These included Dr Constantine Hering (1800–80), who formulated the 'laws of cure', explaining how symptoms affect organ systems and move from one part of the body to another as a cure occurs. Dr James Tyler Kent (1849–1916) introduced the idea of constitutional types, which is now the basis of classical homeopathy, and advocated the use of high potency remedies.

In the later years of the 19th century, a fundamental split occurred in the practice of homeopathy, which was brought about by Dr Richard Hughes (1836–1902), who worked in London and Brighton. He insisted that physical symptoms and the nature of the disease itself was the important factor rather than the holistic approach based on the make-up of the whole individual person. Hughes rejected the concept of constitutional types and advocated the use of low potency remedies. Although he worked as a homeopath, his approach was to attempt to make homeopathy more scientific and to bring it closer to the practices of conventional medicine. Some other homeopathic doctors followed the approach of Hughes, and the split led to a collapse in faith in the whole practice of homeopathy during the earlier part of the 20th century. As the 20th century advanced, however, homeopathy regained its following and respect. Conventional medicine and homeopathy have continued to advance, and there is now a greater sympathy and understanding between the practitioners in both these important disciplines.